THE FILM OF
MURDER IN THE CATHEDRAL

THE WOODEN CRUCIFIX IN THE ARCHBISHOP'S HALL

THE FILM OF

MURDER IN THE CATHEDRAL

by

T. S. ELIOT

and

GEORGE HOELLERING

FABER AND FABER LIMITED

24 Russell Square, London, W.C.1

First published in mcmlii
by Faber and Faber Limited
24 Russell Square London W.C.1
Printed in Great Britain by
R. MacLehose and Company Limited
The University Press Glasgow

The drawings in this book are sketches for the film made by Peter Pendrey.

The photographs on Plates 1-40 are by Angus McBean. The following eight plates of small stills are enlargements from the negative of the actual film.

CARVED PANEL FROM THE MAIN DOOR OF THE CATHEDRAL

PREFACE BY T. S. ELIOT

Murder in the Cathedral is, I believe, the first contemporary verse play to be adapted to the screen. That is in itself a justification for publishing this film script, apart from the value and interest of the illustrative matter. It is certainly the only excuse for a preface by the author of the play.

I should like, first of all, to make clear the limits of my collaboration. At the beginning, Mr. Hoellering asked me to make a film recording of the entire play in my own voice. This recording (which was only completed after a number of sessions) was to serve as a guide, for himself and for the actors, to the rhythms and emphases of the verse as I heard it myself. He tells me that he found this recording very useful: I only know that it suggested to him the possibility of using my voice for the words of the Fourth Tempter—after he had had the happy idea of presenting the Fourth Temptation merely as a voice proceeding from an invisible actor. (He did wisely in demanding of me another recording of this voice, made later after the filming of the scene: for no one—certainly not the author—can throw himself completely into any one part, when he is reading all the parts in succession).

After making this first recording, I wrote the preliminary scenes which he told me would be needed to turn the play into an intelligible film. He gave me the subject-matter of these scenes: I had only to provide the words. Of the necessity of these additional scenes I shall have something to say presently. As to the quality of the verse, I should like to say this: that if it seems inferior to that of the original play, I must ask the critic to observe that I had to imitate a style which I had abandoned as unsuitable for other purposes than that of this one play; and that to compose a pastiche of one's own work some years later is almost as difficult as to imitate the work of another writer. If the new lines are judged to be as good as the old ones, that may call into question the value of the play itself as a contribution to poetry; but I shall nevertheless conclude that the additions constitute a successful *tour de force*.

Beyond the execution of these two definite tasks, my collaboration in the making of the film seems to have been limited to frequent discussions with the producer, in which I accepted nearly all of his suggestions, to frequent visits to the workshop and the studio, and one or two lengthy arguments where differences of opinion arose. Such occasions were rare. I learned something about film technique. And, just as, in learning a foreign language, we learn more about the resources and limitations of our own, so I think that I learned something more about the theatre, in discovering the different resources and limitations of the screen.

The first and most obvious difference, I found, was that the cinema (even where fantasy is introduced) is much more realistic than the stage. Especially in an historical picture, the setting, the costume, and the way of life represented have to be accurate. Even a minor anachronism is intolerable. On the stage much can be overlooked or forgiven; and indeed, an excessive care for accuracy of historical detail can become burdensome and distracting. In watching a stage performance, the member of the audience is in direct contact with the actor, is always conscious that he is looking at a stage and listening to an actor playing a part. In looking at a film, we are much more passive; as audience, we contribute less. We are seized with the illusion that we are observing the actual event, or at least a series of photographs of the actual event; and nothing must be allowed to break this illusion. Hence the precise attention to detail given by Mr. Hoellering, an attention which at first seemed to me excessive. In the theatre, the first problem to present itself is likely to be that of casting. For the Film of 'Murder in the Cathedral', Mr. Hoellering's first care was that the materials for the costumes should be woven in exactly the same way, from exactly the same materials, as they would have been in the twelfth century. I came to appreciate the importance of texture of material, and the kinds of folds into which the material falls, when fashioned into garments and worn by the actors, after I had seen the first photographing.

The difference between stage and screen in respect of realism is so great, I think, as to be a difference of kind rather than degree. It does not indicate any superiority of either medium over the other: it is merely a difference. It has further consequences. The film, standing in a different relation to reality from that of the stage, demands rather different treatment of *plot*. An intricate plot, intelligible on the stage, might be completely mystifying on the screen. The audience has no time to think back, to establish relations between early hints and subsequent discoveries. The picture passes before the eyes too quickly; and

8

CARVED PANEL FROM THE MAIN DOOR OF THE CATHEDRAL

there are no intervals in which to take stock of what has happened, and make conjectures of what is going to happen. The observer is, as I have said, in a more passive state. The film seems to me to be nearer to narrative and to depend much more upon the episodic. And, as the observer is in a more passive state of mind than if he were watching a stage play, so he has to have more explained to him. When Mr. Hoellering pointed out to me that the situation at the beginning of the play of 'Murder in the Cathedral' needed some preliminary matter to make it intelligible, I at first supposed that what he had in mind was that a film was aimed at a much larger, and therefore less well informed audience, ignorant of English history, than that which goes to see a stage play. I very soon became aware that it was not a difference between one type of audience and another, but between two different dramatic forms. The additional scenes, to explain the background of events, are essential for *any* audience, including even those persons already familiar with the play. On the other hand, I hope that no amateur stage producer will ever be so ill-advised as to add these scenes to his production. They are right for the film; they would ruin the shape of the play. In the play, there is not room, beside Thomas Becket, for another dominating character such as Henry II; but in the film, he is not only admissible, but necessary.

I then discovered another interesting and important difference. The speeches of my Four Knights, which in the play are addressed directly to the audience, had to be completely revised. (Mr. Hoellering himself is responsible for the ingenious rearrangement and abbreviation; and I am responsible only for the words of the new ending of the scene.) This also is a consequence of the *realism* of film: the *Stilbruch*—as such an abrupt change is aptly called in German—would be intolerable. (It took me some time, and much persuasion, to understand the difference, and accept it.) For one thing, the camera *must never stand still*. An audience can give their attention to four men actually speaking to them; but to look at the picture of the same four men for that length of time would be an intolerable strain. Furthermore, having once got away from the scene of the murder, it would be impossible to get back to it. Therefore the speeches have to be adapted so as to be spoken to the crowd assembled at the cathedral; and when the third knight turns at last to address the audience, he must make his point very quickly and clearly, so that his hearers may return at once to the illusion of being eye-witnesses of an event which took place nearly eight hundred years ago.

In looking at a film we are always under *direction of the eye*. It is part of the problem of the producer, to decide to what point on the screen, at every moment, the eyes of the audience are to be directed. You are, in fact, looking at the picture, though you do not realise it, through the eyes of the producer. What you see is what he makes the camera see. The fact that the audience's vision is directed by the producer of the film has special consequences for a verse play. It is important, first, that what you see should never distract your attention from what you hear. I believe this presented Mr. Hoellering with some of his most difficult problems. No one perhaps but I, who followed the creation of the film from beginning to end, can appreciate these difficulties, and Mr. Hoellering's success in solving them. Several visual effects, magnificent in themselves, were sacrificed because he was convinced that the audience in watching them would cease to attend to the words. Second, the fact that the illustration of the words by the scene is, so much more positively than on the stage, an interpretation of the meaning of the words, points to the conclusion that only a producer who understands poetry, and has taken a good deal of trouble to grasp the value of every line, is competent to deal with such a play at all. If the production of this film of 'Murder in the Ca- thedral' leads—as I hope it may—to further experiment in the cinema with verse by living poets (and with plays written by poets *for* the cinema, not merely adaptations from the stage) the results can only be successful where there has been close co-operation and understanding between author and producer.

The play was originally written to be performed under the special conditions of the Chapter House at Canterbury, accepting the limitations and exploiting the special advantages of such a setting. Allowing for the great differences of aim and technique between stage and screen, I think that in some respects— notably in the treatment of the choral passages—this film version makes the meaning clearer, and in that way is nearer to what the play would have been, had it been written for the London theatre and by a dramatist of greater ex- perience. I leave Mr. Hoellering to draw attention to some of the changes and developments from the producer's point of view.

T. S. ELIOT

JEWELLERY, HAND-WOVEN MATERIALS, A CROOK AND A CROSS
MADE FOR THE ARCHBISHOP

PREFACE BY GEORGE HOELLERING

It is not an altogether easy task for me to draw attention, as Mr. Eliot has asked me to do, to the main differences between the stage and screen versions of *Murder in the Cathedral*. The reason is that I did not approach Mr. Eliot's text as that of a stage play. I saw in it a great dramatic poem, which had a definite literary form but was 'open' as far as its adaptation to any other medium was concerned. As a film director, I am grateful that in writing *Murder in the Cathedral* Mr. Eliot was obliged to keep in mind conditions of production different from those of the normal stage. It was, of course, written for a particular occasion—for a performance at the Chapter House, Canterbury, as he states in his preface—but to my mind it was just as far removed from the ordinary stage as from the screen, and it was this that attracted me about it. Had the play been written with the requirements of the theatrical stage more strictly in mind, I would have had far less of an incentive for transferring it to the screen: I could only have spoilt something that was already perfect in its own way.

As it was, I considered *Murder in the Cathedral* one of the most successful and important dramatic poems of our time. My task was to transfer it to the screen with all its literary qualities intact, and with the minimum changes necessary to allow these qualities to emerge successfully on the screen. Before dealing with the details of this adaptation, I should like, however, to state what I consider the main relevant differences between theatre and film.

The theatre is a mature art form. Film is a very recent invention, and one that is still in process of development. Whatever is seen on the stage is real; everything seen on the screen is, in a sense, an optical illusion. Yet film is the more realistic medium of the two. This may be explained by the following considerations: in the theatre, what the spectator sees is always a 'total shot', never a detail. Film, as the more flexible medium, can lead the spectator from a total view to the smallest detail (in a close-up), and back again. The actor does not need to speak up to the gallery, he can use his natural voice. And while, on the stage, he must address himself to the entire audience, to many eyes and ears at the same time, in a film his words and gestures are directed at individual persons. The camera and the microphone are the eyes and ears of each individual spectator (for example, an actor looking straight into the camera looks, from the screen, at *you personally*, not at the audience in general). And finally, while a stage performance varies even with the same cast, a film performance is final and definite—a point of special importance in the case of the present film, where the performances that are seen on the screen were approved not only by the director, but by the author.

The silent film was entirely a visual art. Narration was made coherent by the use of interspersed titles, but the best films were those that needed the least number of titles. This had the effect of turning film, from the very beginning, into a director's medium. When sound was invented, film became an aural as well as a visual art, and the captions were replaced by dialogue. The writer's contribution now became more important, but the influence of the director and the producer still remained paramount, and the writer had very little say in the whole matter.

When sound first became available, I was more interested in the opportunities it provided for musical accompaniment than in dialogue. In my first sound film, *Hortobagy*, I was lucky enough to gain a musician of the calibre of Mr. Laszlo Lajtha (who also wrote the music for *Murder in the Cathedral*) as collaborator. He was able to complete the visual part of the film by a musical score which ranged all the way from the most primitive horn sounds through folk songs and dances to the most complex orchestral music, and the need for dialogue was thus reduced to a minimum. After *Hortobagy*, however, I began to look for a subject which would allow me to combine words and images in the same way in which I had previously combined images and music. My attention very soon turned to poetic drama, as it is only there that one can find dialogue which also partakes of some of the qualities of music, and my choice finally fell on Mr. Eliot's *Murder in the Cathedral*.

Having studied the play carefully I started on the screen adaptation of the text, and suggested a number of alterations to Mr. Eliot. These were later, with his approval, incorporated in the shooting script. Among them were the following:

1. (Before the opening of the stage play) Mr. Eliot, on my suggestion, wrote the new Court scene and a new women's chorus, which he discusses in his preface, especially for the film, as well as the Prior's speech

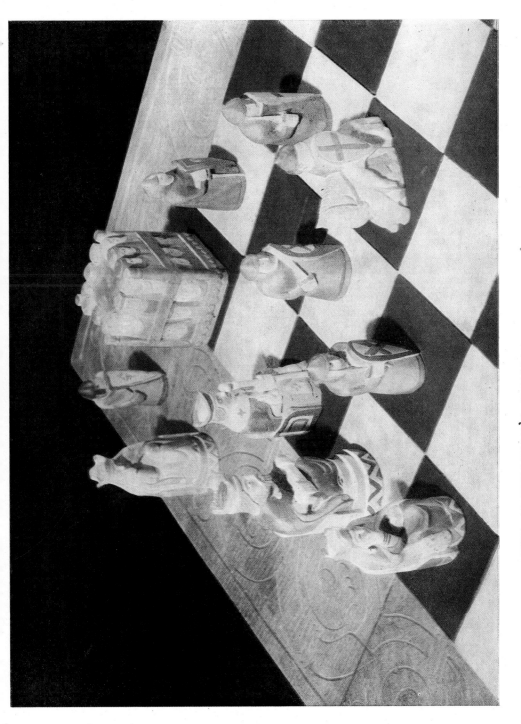

THE ARCHBISHOP'S CHESSBOARD CARVED IN WOOD

to the people of Canterbury, announcing the Archbishop's departure into exile.

The introduction of these new scenes necessitated a new sequence bridging Becket's seven years' exile, beginning with a shot of the sea which now divided the Archbishop from his flock.

2. From here, the film follows the text of the play down to the Fourth Tempter's words 'that the wheel may turn and still/be forever still'. The next passage, 'There is no rest in the house . . .', is spoken by a priest, instead of by the women of Canterbury. Then comes a passage spoken by three tempters, not by all four as in the play, as the Fourth Tempter does not appear on the screen, and the next speech is spoken by one instead of by all the priests. The women's chorus was thus removed from direct contact with the Archbishop, the tempters and the priests in this scene.

The next change is the breaking-up of the chorus 'Does the bird sing in the South . . .' into a dialogue scene, the words being spoken by a simple peasant family, typical of the common people of Canterbury and elsewhere. The scene thus forms a bridge between the Christmas sermon, which marks a radical division in the play, and the next appearance of the priests ('since Christmas a day . . .'). The later chorus, 'I have smelt them, the death-bringers . . .', was also broken up, this time into individual women's voices—a task made easier by the fact that many of the sentences start with 'I'. There follows Becket's speech to the women, where great care was taken not to bring the Archbishop too close to the women visually. When the priests try to drag him away to safety, Becket's words 'Go to vespers . . .' were omitted, so that they could be used in a later scene: when, shortly before the return of the knights, the priests again implore Becket to leave. He tells them to go to vespers, and by blessing them forces them to withdraw, as there is nothing more they can say after having received his blessing. This handling of the scene greatly increases its dramatic intensity, as the Archbishop faces his murderers alone, instead of having around him a number of priests who do not lift a finger to come to his aid. This, in my opinion, is an improvement which could also be used in stage productions of the play.

The next major alteration is the radical reduction of the knights' speeches, and the insertion of a new speech specially written by Mr. Eliot. This change was necessary because it had been found that in stage productions these speeches

13

amused the audience instead of shocking them, and thereby made them miss the point—the main point of the whole play. Whether the new speech will achieve the intended effect, I do not know; people are very difficult to shock these days. But at least it will give them something to think about.

All the priests' speeches following those of the knights were removed, as they were suitable for a church, but not for a stage or screen production. The point that the Archbishop, through his murder, has become a saint, had to be handled much more discreetly; it could not be directly stated in a speech closely following on the murder. What happens is that the knights disappear before the approaching procession carrying the Archbishop's body, and only the words of the last chorus, accompanied by suitable music, are heard.

Apart from these particular changes, there is one difference of great importance between the film and the play: the handling of the women's chorus. From the moment of their first appearance, the women are shown as real women of Canterbury, praying at the altar of the Virgin, going about their work, etc. They have been completely integrated with the action of the play, in a way which it would be impossible to achieve on the stage. This has the effect of tightening the whole story of the film and thereby heightens the spectator's interest in the action.

The main problem of the entire production was to find the right balance between dialogue and picture, and thus to allow Mr. Eliot's poetry to make its maximum impact on the screen. This was achieved by a close and genuine collaboration between author and director, and I should like *Murder in the Cathedral* to be regarded as an experiment in a new type of film, where dialogue is at last given an equal place to picture, and where the audience is called upon to listen as well as to look.

GEORGE HOELLERING

EMBROIDERED BANNERS OF ST. STEPHEN, ST. JOHN, AND THE HOLY INNOCENTS

MURDER IN THE CATHEDRAL

A Screenplay by T. S. Eliot
Music by Laszlo Lajtha
Produced and Directed by George Hoellering

Script	George Hoellering	*Camera Operator*	Norman Foley
Art Director	Peter Pendrey	*Editor*	Anne Allnatt
Sculpture	Edwin Florence	*Sound Supervisor*	Ken Cameron
Director of Photography	David Kosky	*Sound Mixer*	F. Arnaud

Musical Adviser Ilona Kabos

Music recorded by
The London Philharmonic Orchestra
Conducted by Sir Adrian Boult
and
The Renaissance Singers
Conducted by Michael Howard

Mediæval song sung by Diana Maddox

CAST

Thomas Becket, Archbishop of Canterbury	Father John Groser
King Henry II	Alexander Gauge
First Tempter	David Ward
Second Tempter	George Woodbridge
Third Tempter	Basil Burton
Fourth Tempter spoken by	T. S. Eliot
First Priest	Donald Bisset
Second Priest (Prior)	Clement McCallin
Third Priest	Michael Groser
First Knight	Mark Dignam*
Second Knight	Michael Aldridge*
Third Knight	Leo McKern*
Fourth Knight	Paul Rogers*
Bishop Foliot	Alban Blakelock
Herald	Niall MacGinnis

Women's Chorus:
Led by: Kay Astor, Jill Balcon, Renée Bourne-Webb, Beryl Calder, Ysanne Churchman, Anne
Cullen, Diana Maddox, Jill Nyasa, Mary O'Farrell
with Helen Best, Renée Blakelock, Janet Butler, Bettina Carroll, Margaret Crozier, Olive Gregg,
Viola Johnstone, Kelty McLeod, Martina Mayne, Eileen Vine

The Men:
Pl. H. Alexander, Ernest Bale, Stanley Van Beers, Geoffrey Bellmann, Tom Colmer, Howell
Davies, John Van Eyssen,* Paul Hansard,* Denis Holmes, David Keir, John Kelly, E. J.
Kennedy, Fletcher Lightfoot, Victor Lucas, William Patrick, Charles Peters, Gerald Pring,
Frederick Ross
The Chess Game played in the film was devised by S. Tartakower
* *Appearing by permission of the Old Vic*

Canterbury, 1164

Music is heard
The screen is black
Slowly there appears a crucifix standing in a workshop
    where sculptures and tools are lying about
A priest is painting the foot of the crucifix
A bell is heard ringing
The priest gets up and goes to look out of the window
The music ends
The priest puts on his cloak and goes out of the room

A bell tower
A monk is ringing the bell
He lets go of the rope and it swings backwards and forwards

The crypt
The Archbishop is kneeling at the altar
Behind him kneel priests and monks
The Archbishop rises to address them:

Archbishop Canons and brethren, I am summoned to the King
Who holds his Court at Northampton. Therefore I have
    summoned you—
Since I must be gone by daybreak—to hear me and to learn
The cause, the need, the purpose and the probable end.
You know of John the Marshall, how he would possess
    himself
Of lands appurtenant to a vassal of our see:
You know how we dismissed his suit, finding
No shadow of title. Crafty and mischievous,
He would have taken his case before the King's court
To provoke dissension to his private profit,
Setting on foot great evil, to serve a little gain.
You know that I denied the ground of his appeal
And sent three knights to testify. Therefore I am sum-
    moned.
But this is now no longer
The small adventure of a petty robber
Greedy to gain a manor and a field or two,
A rat slipping into the Church's granary.
The accuser will be the King. The accused will be
Thomas, Archbishop of Canterbury. The forfeit
Is a great power, all power.
                                        Were I to yield,
The Church, all Christendom, Christ in His Vicar
Would suffer limitation. If I stand firm,
It is only I who am diminished and deprived.
Perhaps to exile. Most surely a long absence:
For if no justice here, then justification
In Rome. If I am powerless here, I must invoke
The power of Rome.

But you, remember, and be comforted.
This is no new discord, only one engagement
In an unending war. The obscure chronicle
Of the future when it is the past, will show
The Church brought many times much nearer desolation
And against all Christ's promise.

                                There must be two powers
Always in this world. The King would have one power
    alone
The worldly power which reaches towards the absolute
And even when aiming well, still brings forth evil
And most when absolute, bows down to Anti-Christ.

There is but one absolute King, the Lord you serve.
Pray for me. And in all things be obedient;
Be sober and discreet, restrained and prudent, and observe
Such orders as the Father Prior may give. Receive our
    blessing.

The priests and monks kneel
The Archbishop blesses them and turns to the altar and kneels down
The painting of the Day of Judgement over the altar comes closer until it fills the screen
    while the Choir is heard singing:

Vesper Hymn

Lucis Creator optime,
Lucem dierum proferens,
Primordiis lucis novae
Mundi parans originem:

Ne mens gravata crimine,
Vitae sit exsul munere,
Dum nil perenne cogitat,
Seseque culpis illigat.

Praesta, Pater pissime,
Patrique compar Unice,
Cum Spiritu Paraclito,
Regnans per omne saeculum. Amen.

Early morning
The face of the Virgin
Slowly the Mary Chapel appears
Women kneel before the painting of the Virgin and Child
Lighted candles stand at the Virgin's feet
The women pray for the Archbishop:

Chorus of Women	Here let us kneel, close by the cathedral. Here let us pray for our good Archbishop;
	may his journey be easy, his road be smooth, weather and wind be fair, may his horse not fail.
	God who created us
	Jesus who saved us
	Spirit who cleanseth us
	God be with you between the woods
	Jesus be with you at the turning of the hill
	Spirit be with you in crossing the stream
	Blessed Mary, St. Michael, St. Elphege, and all the saints pray.
	May the prayers of the poor, of your poor people, your poor folk of Kent, avail,
	And of us, the women of Canterbury. Now
	May the King be enlightened, your enemies thwarted, the truth prevail, all powers of evil driven away.
One Woman	But this morning my fire would not kindle
Another Woman	This morning my cauldron would not boil
A third Woman	Last night I was ridden by witches
	And the cat jumped onto the bed
A fourth Woman	Our housedog howled all the night
	At the owl that cried in the elmtree
A fifth Woman	My wedding ring slipped from my finger
	And my milk jug fell on the hearth.
A sixth Woman	O Lord Archbishop, do not carry the cross, or the cross will carry you. I have boding of bane and bale. Return, return to us, for without you we have no succour or stay.

Music is heard

The screen is black
Rays of light fall across the screen and the crucifix is seen from the side hanging on the wall
A broad track coming down a hill
The sky is dark and cloudy
Four knights on horseback gallop down the hill
The head of the crucifix
A shadow falls over Christ's face
A way through the fields where the wayside cross stands.
It is early morning.
The Archbishop and three knights ride away
A cock crows three times
A mediaeval animal carved on the capital of a pillar
The King's Court
The bishops and nobles enter in a double file, followed by the King
Two axemen look down from the windows
The King makes a sign   The music ends
The Archbishop and his three knights walk in, to the sound of a fanfare
The Archbishop bows and addresses the King

24

Archbishop My Lord the King, I am guilty of no treason. Never would
I be lacking in reverence for the King's Grace or for
the King's Law in his domain. The suit of John the
Marshal pertained to my court; it was tried in my
court; and it was dismissed. The evidence was plain,
the judgement that imposed by canon law. Beyond that
court there could be no appeal, for such a case, in this
land. Therefore, when summoned to your court, I
could not comply: that were to fail in my duty as
Archbishop and betray the Church in all Christendom. Yet I did not fail in respect for the King's
Majesty: I sent three of my knights to give account of
actions, to testify that this suit could not be allowed,
and to explain my absence. More I could not do.

King Your defence is not accepted. You pretend to ignore the
Constitutions of Clarendon. To these every bishop, all
of them here present, consented, and you too, my Lord
Archbishop. The Constitutions admit that a plaintiff
has the right of appeal from the Archdeacon to the
Bishop, from the Bishop to the Archbishop, and from
the Archbishop to the King. I therefore hold you
guilty of treason. And I shall hold guilty of treason
all those—if there be any—who support you in this
conduct. My Lords Bishops, I demand that you now
pronounce the judgement of my Council.

A few seconds' silence.

First Bishop What shall we say?

Second Bishop To my mind, the question is perfectly simple. We signed
the Constitutions of Clarendon. We are honest men;
the oath was binding; and for us to break it now
would be excessively imprudent.

Third Bishop	The Archbishop exceeds his authority. I refuse to be bullied. I say we should pronounce for the King.
Fourth Bishop	But the saving clause—Thomas consented saving only the law of the Church.
First Bishop	And the King did not accept this reservation.
Fifth Bishop	So Thomas refused to sign.
Sixth Bishop	For my part, I am convinced that the true interests of the Church demand that we should give judgement for the King. It was the King who forced Becket upon us as Archbishop against our wishes and the interests of the Church. He must now regret this interference. By condemning Thomas we shall be expressing, in the clearest possible manner, our objection to the intrusion of the State into Church affairs.
Third Bishop	I agree. And then we can have My Lord of London as Archbishop—a choice, my Lords, which I know we should all have preferred.
Bishop Foliot	My Lord, you are too kind.
Second Bishop	Yes, my Lord, we know you for the wisest man among us, and a moderate man, an extremely moderate man.
Bishop Foliot	I think I see a way.
Seventh Bishop	But I am fearful of hasty measures. It is most inconvenient, but Thomas is still Archbishop, and has power of excommunication over us.
Bishop Foliot	I know, I know, and that is why I shall propose this solution, which will make it possible for us to satisfy the King.
	Voices sink to an indistinct murmur.

First Noble	This is better than a tournament (*Laughter*).
Second Noble	And the onlookers, my Lord, see the best of the game.
Third Noble	Look at those bishops! like frightened birds when one of my falcons is ranging, they don't know where to turn.
Fourth Noble	These are birds too fat to fly.
Fifth Noble	This is an end to Bishop's Law, I think: tomorrow there will be only King's Law.
Second Noble	Then tomorrow, my Lord, look to your own rights.
Sixth Noble	Ay, ay, one thing at a time. Let King eat Bishop, he'll find his loyal barons tougher meat.
Seventh Noble	I do not like it, I tell you. The King may grow too powerful for us.
Seventh Bishop	My Lord of Canterbury, we, the bishops of this realm, hold that you have failed of the respect due to the King's Grace. By reason of your oath of homage, you were bound, saving only urgent business or infirmity, to answer the King's summons in person. This you failed to do: we exhort you, therefore, to admit your contumacy, and throw yourself upon the King's mercy.
Some Nobles	Hear, hear.
Archbishop	My Lord King, there is no subtlety in this charge, and I will use no subtlety in my defence. I am not guilty. Were I to give any other answer, then should I three times break faith. The oath I took at Clarendon was ever saving my order; that all men know. Should I now be faithless to my vows as priest and bishop? These same Constitutions of Clarendon were then annulled by the Pope. Should I now be faithless to my obedience to the Vicar of Christ?

And, as touching the third bond, I know well what evils would come

29

upon this country of England, were I to suffer
unprotesting the subjection of the spiritual power to
the temporal. Should I now be faithless to my people?
My Lords, as concerning the temporal power, though it be
also of God, as signified in the consecration of the
King to his office when he is anointed and crowned by
the Church, I bid you think that this same temporal
power has to do with today and tomorrow. Those
who wield it, as you, my Lords, wield this power under
the King, are much tempted to bend it to their own
advantage. You think of estates and honours for
yourselves and for your sons: yet it is but a little while,
and your estates are scattered, and your honours lost,
and your monuments broken, and your names forgotten.
Tomorrow where is Vere? where is Bohun? Where is . . .
You would do well to remember the Church of God
which was, and is and ever shall be to the end of the
world according to the promises of Christ.
But for you, my Lords Bishops, my heart is very sorrowful.
You have deserted me to whom you are bound by your
order, by your estate and by your dignity. Those
disciples, that were afterwards Saints by the Grace of
the Holy Spirit, left Our Lord and fled through bodily
fear: take heed that you do not desert me through the
greater sin of worldly greed and ambition, and that no
saving grace redeem your end.
There is one here would willingly be Archbishop in my
stead.
Consider, my Lords, that what violates the Law of God
cannot be lawful. Consider, that the King's reverence
cannot be magnified by abating the reverence of the

31

Church. You have yet time, and the time is this very moment and no more, to abjure your apostasy and renew your obedience to the Law of Christ's Church, to Christ's Vicar, and to me.

And for myself, though I stand alone in England, though every deprivation and enforcement ensue to me, yet will I in no way relinquish the right.

King (shouts) Hear him no further, but pronounce! I have not got you here to whisper and whine, to plead with an Archbishop, but to give judgement upon a manifest and shameless traitor. Will you make yourselves accomplices of this man? I have consulted you according to the form of law: what more do you require? Pronounce judgement, or by the Mass, I will strip you, every one of you, out of palace and church; ay, out of chasuble and cassock, too.

First Bishop My Lord! we are taken between the hammer and the anvil: have mercy upon us!

Archbishop Fool! you betray yourself among irreverent laughing men. You ask me to commit a greater sin, to confirm and justify you in your cowardice. The law of man that breaks the law of God is no law, but lawless violence.

Betray me if you will, but do not ask me to betray.

Bishop Foliot My Lord the King. I have taken counsel with my brethren here gathered, and they have asked me to put forward a proposal which should satisfy both Your Majesty's reasonable demand and their own not unreasonable scruples. The Archbishop, as our metropolitan, forbids us to proceed further with this case.

Here, it must be admitted, he is acting according to the strict letter of ecclesiastical law, however we may interpret his

32

motives. He has the power of excommunication over us; and I think your Majesty will acknowledge, that it would be a very grave scandal, and the excuse for misconduct among the common people, for the whole of your bench of bishops to be excommunicated. There is nothing that we more earnestly desire, than to demonstrate our loyalty to Your Majesty's person and Your Majesty's laws. We therefore respectfully propose to appeal to the Pope to release us from our canonical obedience to the Archbishop: we shall then be in a position to pronounce judgement upon him. I hope that this suggestion will commend itself to Your Majesty.

King Cowards and traitors! I will have judgement, and I will have it now.

(To the nobles): You have heard these wind-bags and precise committee men. You, my Lords, are men of action, who can prove your loyalty without palaver. Pronounce the judgement.

Noble My Lord Archbishop, we declare you guilty of ...

Archbishop What is this? Did I not say truly that the law of man that violates the law of God is no law, but lawlessness? You respect not even these same Constitutions of Clarendon that the King invokes. Is it not there affirmed that offences by the clergy against the King shall be punished by the Church? You are but lay persons: you can utter no judgement upon your Father in God. I will not hear you.

The Archbishop leaves the court followed by his knights

Music is heard while women walk through the main Cathedral
    doors
The carved figure of Christ over the door comes closer until it
    fills the screen

The Prior stands in the transept surrounded by priests and the
Archbishop's knights
He speaks to the people:

  Prior My brethren, and you, good people of Canterbury.
           These knights have brought bad news: bad news is what I
               give you.
           The King's Court has given judgement: if that is a judgement
           Which is only the voice of the wicked and the frightened;

34

And if that is a Court, which has no authority
To pronounce such a judgement. The Archbishop is gone.
He refused to hear the sentence, left the Court.
He has taken ship for France, for what can he do
But appeal to the Holy Father, to the judgement seat of
    Rome?
He is not a man who has fled for his own safety—
Safety he could have bought, at the price of betrayal—
But he is your Archbishop, who must carry on the fight
Where the fight can be waged, no other place than Rome.
To Rome he will appeal, for the Church in England,
For the law of God in England. He will return to you
With the Holy Father's blessing, and the Papal anathema.
For us is but to wait, to pray, to suffer
Perhaps for a long time. I have nothing to promise you
Until his return, but waiting and suffering.
I have nothing to ask of you but prayer and endurance.
The men at arms will soon be here
To enforce the King's command, to confirm the seizure
By John the Marshal, to the great harm of some of you;
To take forfeit of us, imposing heavy penalty.
We must not withstand them. You must not withstand
    them.
The Archbishop would not wish of you rebellious behavi-
    our
Against the King, to the danger of your bodies,
Or hatred and anger to the danger of your souls.
We must comply, but not consent. Pray to St. Elphege.
Let us bow the knee. Let us pray.

The Prior kneels
The backs of kneeling people fill the screen
The choir is heard singing the first lines of the Te Deum

The altar in the crypt
A monk is putting out the candles on the altar
When the last candle is extinguished the singing ends

The Sea
A woman's voice is heard singing:

In Rama sonat gemitus, plorante Rachel Anglie:
Herodis namque genitus, dat ipsam ignominie.
En eius primogenitus, et Joseph Cantuarie,
Exul at fisto venditus, Egiptum colit Gallie

The noise of the sea grows louder and drowns the singing
The waves cover the screen

Women walk into the Mary Chapel
They light candles and place them at the foot of the painting of the Virgin
They kneel
The painting comes closer until the heads of the Virgin and child fill the screen
During this sequence women's voices are heard speaking the chorus:

> *Chorus*   Here let us stand, close by the cathedral. Here let us wait.
> Are we drawn by danger? Is it the knowledge of safety,
>   that draws our feet
> Towards the cathedral? What danger can be
> For us, the poor, the poor women of Canterbury? what
>   tribulation
> With which we are not already familiar? There is no
>   danger

For us, and there is no safety in the cathedral. Some presage
        of an act
Which our eyes are compelled to witness, has forced our
        feet
Towards the cathedral. We are forced to bear witness.

Since golden October declined into sombre November
And the apples were gathered and stored, and the land
        became brown sharp points of death in a waste of
        water and mud,
The New Year waits, breathes, waits, whispers in darkness.
While the labourer kicks off a muddy boot and stretches his
        hand to the fire,
The New Year waits, destiny waits for the coming.
Who has stretched out his hand to the fire and remembered
        the Saints at All Hallows,
Remembered the martyrs and saints who wait? and who
        shall
Stretch out his hand to the fire, and deny his master? who
        shall be warm
By the fire, and deny his master?

Seven years and the summer is over
Seven years since the Archbishop left us,
He who was always kind to his people.
But it would not be well if he should return.
King rules or barons rule;
We have suffered various oppression,
But mostly we are left to our own devices,
And we are content if we are left alone.
We try to keep our households in order;

The merchant, shy and cautious, tries to compile a little
    fortune,
And the labourer bends to his piece of earth, earth-colour,
    his own colour,
Preferring to pass unobserved.
Now I fear disturbance of the quiet seasons:
Winter shall come bringing death from the sea,
Ruinous spring shall beat at our doors,
Root and shoot shall eat our eyes and our ears,
Disastrous summer burn up the beds of our streams
And the poor shall wait for another decaying October.
Why should the summer bring consolation
For autumn fires and winter fogs?
What shall we do in the heat of summer
But wait in barren orchards for another October?
Some malady is coming upon us. We wait, we wait,

And the saints and martyrs wait, for those who shall be
    martyrs and saints.
Destiny waits in the hand of God, shaping the still un-
    shapen:
I have seen these things in a shaft of sunlight.
Destiny waits in the hand of God, not in the hands of
    statesmen
Who do, some well, some ill, planning and guessing,
Having their aims which turn in their hands in the pattern
    of time.
Come, happy December, who shall observe you, who
    shall preserve you?
Shall the Son of Man be born again in the litter of scorn?
For us, the poor, there is no action,
But only to wait and to witness.

A flight of steps leading down to the transept
The three priests, deep in conversation, walk down the steps
They are interrupted by the voice of the Messenger who comes through a small archway
  in another corner of the transept
He is surrounded by a crowd of peasants who have followed him into the cathedral
The priests go to the Messenger who bows and addresses them

First Priest Seven years and the summer is over.
          Seven years since the Archbishop left us.
Second Priest What does the Archbishop do, and our Sovereign Lord
              the Pope

          With the stubborn King and the French King
          In ceaseless intrigue, combinations,
          In conference, meetings accepted, meetings refused,
          Meetings unended or endless
          At one place or another in France?
Third Priest I see nothing quite conclusive in the art of temporal
              government,
          But violence, duplicity and frequent malversation.
          King rules or barons rule:
          The strong man strongly and the weak man by caprice.
          They have but one law, to seize the power and keep it,
          And the steadfast can manipulate the greed and lust of
              others,
          The feeble is devoured by his own.
First Priest Shall these things not end
          Until the poor at the gate
          Have forgotten their friend, their Father in God, have
              forgotten
          That they had a friend?

Messenger Servants of God, and watchers of the temple,
I am here to inform you, without circumlocution:
The Archbishop is in England, and is close outside the city.
I was sent before in haste
To give you notice of his coming, as much as was possible,
That you may prepare to meet him.

First Priest What, is the exile ended, is our Lord Archbishop
Reunited with the King? what reconciliation
Of two proud men?

Third Priest   What peace can be found
To grow between the hammer and the anvil?

Second Priest   Tell us,
Are the old disputes at an end, is the wall of pride cast
    down
That divided them? Is it peace or war?

First Priest   Does he come
In full assurance, or only secure
In the power of Rome, the spiritual rule,
The assurance of right, and the love of the people?

Messenger You are right to express a certain incredulity.
He comes in pride and sorrow, affirming all his claims,
Assured, beyond doubt, of the devotion of the people,
Who receive him with scenes of frenzied enthusiasm,
Lining the road and throwing down their capes,
Strewing the way with leaves and late flowers of the season.
The streets of the city will be packed to suffocation,
And I think that his horse will be deprived of its tail,
A single hair of which becomes a precious relic.
He is at one with the Pope, and with the King of France,
Who indeed would have liked to detain him in his king-
    dom:
But as for our King, that is another matter.

42

First Priest But again, is it war or peace?

Messenger   Peace, but not the kiss of peace.
A patched up affair, if you ask my opinion.
And if you ask me, I think the Lord Archbishop
Is not the man to cherish any illusions,
Or yet to diminish the least of his pretensions.
If you ask my opinion, I think that this peace
Is nothing like an end, or like a beginning.
It is common knowledge that when the Archbishop
Parted from the King, he said to the King,
My Lord, he said, I leave you as a man
Whom in this life I shall not see again.
I have this, I assure you, on the highest authority;
There are several opinions as to what he meant,
But no one considers it a happy prognostic.

The Messenger bows to the priests and goes out followed by the peasants

The priests walk back through the transept, discussing the Messenger's news

43

First Priest I fear for the Archbishop, I fear for the Church,
I know that the pride bred of sudden prosperity
Was but confirmed by bitter adversity.
I saw him as Chancellor, flattered by the King,
Liked or feared by courtiers, in their overbearing fashion,
Despised and despising, always isolated,
Never one among them, always insecure;
His pride always feeding upon his own virtues,
Pride drawing sustenance from impartiality,
Pride drawing sustenance from generosity,
Loathing power given by temporal devolution,
Wishing subjection to God alone.
Had the King been greater, or had he been weaker
Things had perhaps been different for Thomas.

Second Priest Yet our lord is returned. Our lord has come back to his
own again.
We have had enough of waiting, from December to
dismal December.
The Archbishop shall be at our head, dispelling dismay
and doubt.
He will tell us what we are to do, he will give us our
orders, instruct us.
Our Lord is at one with the Pope, and also the King of
France.
We can lean on a rock, we can feel a firm foothold
Against the perpetual wash of tides of balance of forces of
barons and landholders.
The rock of God is beneath our feet. Let us meet the
Archbishop with cordial thanksgiving:
Our lord, or Archbishop returns. And when the Arch-
bishop returns
Our doubts are dispelled. Let us therefore rejoice,

I say rejoice, and show a glad face for his welcome.
I am the Archbishop's man. Let us give the Archbishop
    welcome!

Third Priest For good or ill, let the wheel turn.
The wheel has been still, these seven years, and no good.
For ill or good, let the wheel turn.
For who knows the end of good or evil?
Until the grinders cease
And the door shall be shut in the street,
And all the daughters of music shall be brought low.

A monk rings a bell, calling the priests and monks to hear the news
The Archbishop with three followers rides towards Canterbury past the wayside cross
The sky is grey
Three blacksmiths are making a sword in their forge
They heat it in the fire and temper it in a trough of water
They sharpen the sword on a grindstone and look along the blade to see if it is straight
A woman stands in her home spinning flax
Four women work on tapestries showing hunting and harvesting scenes
A bell is heard calling the people to the cathedral
During this sequence women's voices are heard speaking the chorus:

Chorus Here is no continuing city, here is no abiding stay.
Ill the wind, ill the time, uncertain the profit, certain the
     danger.
O late late late, late is the time, late too late, and rotten
     the year;
Evil the wind, and bitter the sea, and grey the sky,
     grey grey grey.
O Thomas, return, Archbishop; return, return to France.
Return. Quickly. Quietly. Leave us to perish in quiet.
You come with applause, you come with rejoicing, but
     you come bringing death into Canterbury:
A doom on the house, a doom on yourself, a doom on
     the world.

We do not wish anything to happen.
Seven years we have lived quietly,
Succeeding in avoiding notice,
Living and partly living.
There have been oppression and luxury,
There have been poverty and licence,
There has been minor injustice.
Yet we have gone on living,
Living and partly living.
Sometimes the corn has failed us,
Sometimes the harvest is good,
One year is a year of rain,
Another a year of dryness,
One year the apples are abundant,
Another year the plums are lacking.
Yet we have gone on living,
Living and partly living.

We have kept the feasts, heard the masses,
We have brewed beer and cyder,
Gathered wood against the winter,
Talked at the corner of the fire,
Talked at the corner of streets,
Talked not always in whispers,
Living and partly living.
We have seen births, deaths and marriages,
We have had various scandals,
We have been afflicted with taxes,
We have had laughter and gossip,
Several girls have disappeared
Unaccountably, and some not able to.
We have all had our private terrors,
Our particular shadows, our secret fears.
But now a great fear is upon us, a fear not of one but of
       many,
A fear like birth and death, when we see birth and death
       alone
In a void apart. We
Are afraid in a fear which we cannot know, which we
       cannot face, which none understands,
And our hearts are torn from us, our brains unskinned
       like the layers of an onion, our selves are lost lost
In a final fear which none understands. O Thomas
       Archbishop,
O Thomas our Lord, leave us and leave us be, in our
       humble and tarnished frame of existence, leave us; do
       not ask us
To stand to the doom on the house, the doom on the
       Archbishop, the doom on the world.

Archbishop, secure and assured of your fate, unaffrayed
among the shades, do you realise what you ask, do
you realise what it means

To the small folk drawn into the pattern of fate, the small
folk who live among small things,

The strain on the brain of the small folk who stand to the
doom of the house, the doom of their lord, the doom
of the world?

O Thomas, Archbishop, leave us, leave us, leave sullen
Dover, and set sail for France. Thomas our Archbishop still our Archbishop even in France. Thomas
Archbishop, set the white sail between the grey sky
and the bitter sea, leave us, leave us for France.

The transept, where monks and a crowd of people have gathered
The women walk forward, speaking the last lines of the chorus
The second priest addresses them angrily:

        Second Priest What a way to talk at such a juncture!
                      You are foolish, immodest and babbling women.
                      Do you not know that the good Archbishop
                      Is likely to arrive at any moment?
                      The crowds in the streets will be cheering and cheering,
                      You go on croaking like frogs in the treetops:
                      But frogs at least can be cooked and eaten.
                      Whatever you are afraid of, in your craven apprehension,
                      Let me ask you at the least to put on pleasant faces,
                      And give a hearty welcome to our good Archbishop.

The Archbishop's voice is heard
The people turn their heads in surprise
The Archbishop walks into the transept and addresses the second priest

Thomas	Peace. And let them be, in their exaltation.

Thomas Peace. And let them be, in their exaltation.
They speak better than they know, and beyond your
    understanding.
They know and do not know, what it is to act or suffer.
They know and do not know, that action is suffering
And suffering is action. Neither does the agent suffer
Nor the patient act. But both are fixed
In an eternal action, an eternal patience
To which all must consent that it may be willed
And which all must suffer that they may will it,
That the pattern may subsist, for the pattern is the action
And the suffering, that the wheel may turn and still
Be forever still.

Second Priest O my Lord, forgive me, I did not see you coming,
Engrossed by the chatter of these foolish women.
Forgive us, my Lord, you would have had a better welcome
If we had been sooner prepared for the event.
But your Lordship knows that seven years of waiting,
Seven years of prayer, seven years of emptiness,
Have better prepared our hearts for your coming,
Than seven days could make ready Canterbury.
However, I will have fires laid in all your rooms
To take the chill off our English December,
Your Lordship now being used to a better climate.
Your Lordship will find your rooms in order as you left
    them.

Thomas And will try to leave them in order as I find them.
I am more than grateful for all your kind attentions.
These are small matters. Little rest in Canterbury
With eager enemies restless about us.
Rebellious bishops, York, London, Salisbury,
Would have intercepted our letters,

Filled the coast with spies and sent to meet me
Some who hold me in bitterest hate.
By God's grace aware of their prevision
I sent my letters on another day,
Had fair crossing, found at Sandwich
Broc, Warenne, and the Sheriff of Kent,
Those who had sworn to have my head from me
Only John, the Dean of Salisbury,
Fearing for the King's name, warning against treason,
Made them hold their hands. So for the time
We are unmolested.

First Priest   But do they follow after?

Thomas For a little time the hungry hawk
Will only soar and hover, circling lower,
Waiting excuse, pretence, opportunity.
End will be simple, sudden, God-given.
Meanwhile the substance of our first act
Will be shadows, and the strife with shadows.
Heavier the interval than the consummation.
All things prepare the event. Watch.

The Archbishop leaves the transept, blessing the kneeling people as he goes

The Archbishop's Hall
The Archbishop comes in and walks through the hall into his chapel
He kneels before the altar
The First Tempter appears

First Tempter You see, my Lord, I do not wait upon ceremony:
                Here I have come, forgetting all acrimony,
                Hoping that your present gravity
                Will find excuse for my humble levity
                Remembering all the good time past.

The screen becomes black
A chess board appears

53

The tempter makes the first move and says:

Your Lordship won't despise an old friend out of favour?
Old Tom, gay Tom, Becket of London,
Your Lordship won't forget that evening on the river
When the King, and you and I were all friends together?
Friendship should be more than biting Time can sever.
What, my Lord, now that you recover
Favour with the King, shall we say that summer's over
Or that the good time cannot last?
Fluting in the meadows, viols in the hall,
Laughter and apple-blossom floating on the water,
Singing at nightfall, whispering in chambers,
Fires devouring the winter season,
Eating up the darkness, with wit and wine and wisdom!
Now that the King and you are in amity,
Clergy and laity may return to gaiety,
Mirth and sportfulness need not walk warily.

Thomas You talk of seasons that are past. I remember
Not worth forgetting.

Tempter	And of the new season.
	Spring has come in winter. Snow in the branches
	Shall float as sweet as blossoms. Ice along the ditches
	Mirror the sunlight. Love in the orchard
	Send the sap shooting. Mirth matches melancholy.
Thomas	We do not know very much of the future
	Except that from generation to generation
	The same things happen again and again.
	Men learn little from others' experience.
	But in the life of one man, never
	The same time returns. Sever
	The cord, shed the scale. Only
	The fool, fixed in his folly, may think
	He can turn the wheel on which he turns.
Tempter	My Lord, a nod is as good as a wink,
	A man will often love what he spurns.
	For the good times past, that are come again
	I am your man.
Thomas	Not in this train
	Look to your behaviour. You were safer
	Think of penitence and follow your master.
Tempter	Not at this gait!
	If you go so fast, others may go faster.
	Your Lordship is too proud!
	The safest beast is not the one that roars most loud,
	This was not the way of the King our master!
	You were not used to be so hard upon sinners
	When they were your friends. Be easy, man!
	The easy man lives to eat the best dinners.
	Take a friend's advice. Leave well alone,
	Or your goose may be cooked and eaten to the bone.
Thomas	You come twenty years too late.

Tempter Then I leave you to your fate.
I leave you to the pleasures of your higher vices,
Which will have to be paid for at higher prices.

The Archbishop checkmates the Tempter
The Tempter gets up and says:

Farewell, my Lord, I do not wait upon ceremony,
I leave as I came, forgetting all acrimony,
Hoping that your present gravity
Will find excuse for my humble levity.
If you will remember me, my Lord, at your prayers,
I'll remember you at kissing-time below the stairs.

Thomas Leave-well-alone, the springtime fancy,
So one thought goes whistling down the wind.
The impossible is still temptation.
The impossible, the undesirable,
Voices under sleep, waking a dead world,
So that the mind may not be whole in the present.

The light goes out on the chess board

The Second Tempter appears at the entrance to the Archbishop's Hall
He bows and comes towards the Archbishop who stands beneath the crucifix

Second Tempter   Your Lordship has forgotten me, perhaps. I will remind
                   you.

We met at Clarendon, at Northampton,
And last at Montmirail, in Maine. Now that I have re-
    called them,
Let us but set these not too pleasant memories
In balance against other, earlier
And weightier ones: those of the Chancellorship.
See how the late ones rise! You, master of policy
Whom all acknowledged, should guide the state again.

Thomas   Your meaning?

Tempter   The Chancellorship that you resigned
When you were made Archbishop—that was a mistake
On your part—still may be regained. Think, my Lord,
Power obtained grows to glory,
Life lasting, a permanent possession.
A templed tomb, monument of marble.
Rule over men reckon no madness.

Thomas   To the man of God what gladness?

Tempter   Sadness
Only to those giving love to God alone.
Shall he who held the solid substance
Wander waking with deceitful shadows?
Power is present. Holiness hereafter.

Thomas   Who then?

Tempter   The Chancellor. King and Chancellor.
King commands. Chancellor richly rules.
This is a sentence not taught in the schools.
To set down the great, protect the poor,
Beneath the throne of God can man do more?
Disarm the ruffian, strengthen the laws,
Rule for the good of the better cause,
Dispensing justice make all even,
Is thrive on earth, and perhaps in heaven.

Thomas	What means?
Tempter	Real power
	Is purchased at price of a certain submission.
	Your spiritual power is earthly perdition.
	Power is present, for him who will wield.
Thomas	Who shall have it?
Tempter	He who will come.
Thomas	What shall be the month?
Tempter	The last from the first.
Thomas	What shall we give for it?
Tempter	Pretence of priestly power.
Thomas	Why should we give it?
Tempter	For the power and the glory.
Thomas	No!
Tempter	Yes! Or bravery will be broken,
	Cabined in Canterbury, realmless ruler,
	Self-bound servant of a powerless Pope,
	The old stag, circled with hounds.
Thomas	No!
Tempter	Yes! men must manœuvre. Monarchs also,
	Waging war abroad, need fast friends at home.
	Private policy is public profit;
	Dignity still shall be dressed with decorum.
Thomas	You forget the bishops
	Whom I have laid under excommunication.
Tempter	Hungry hatred
	Will not strive against intelligent self-interest.
Thomas	You forget the barons. Who will not forget
	Constant curbing of petty privilege.
Tempter	Against the barons
	Is King's cause, churl's cause, Chancellor's cause.

Thomas   No! shall I, who keep the keys
           Of heaven and hell, supreme alone in England,
           Who bind and loose, with power from the Pope,
           Descend to desire a punier power?
           Delegate to deal the doom of damnation,
           To condemn kings, not serve among their servants,
           Is my open office. No! Go.

Tempter   Then I leave you to your fate.
           Your sin soars sunward, covering kings' falcons.

The Tempter goes away
A carved mediaeval animal appears
Music is heard

Thomas   Temporal power, to build a good world,
           To keep order, as the world knows order.
           Those who put their faith in worldly order
           Not controlled by the order of God,
           In confident ignorance, but arrest disorder,
           Make it fast, breed fatal disease,
           Degrade what they exalt. Power with the King—
           I *was* the King, his arm, his better reason.
           But what was once exaltation.
           Would now be only mean descent.

The Archbishop bows to the crucifix and walks away
Clouds move across a grey sky
The Archbishop walks to a window in another corner of his hall and looks out
Women kneel by the wayside cross
Suddenly the Third Tempter appears behind the Archbishop

Third Tempter I am an unexpected visitor.
      Thomas   I expected you.
      Tempter But not in this guise, or for my present purpose.
      Thomas No purpose brings surprise.

Tempter   Well, my Lord,
I am no trifler, and no politician.
To idle or intrigue at court
I have no skill. I am no courtier.
I know a horse, a dog, a wench;
I know how to hold my estates in order,
A country-keeping lord who minds his own business.
It is we country lords who know the country
And we who know what the country needs.
It is our country. We care for the country.
We are the backbone of the nation.
We, not the plotting parasites
About the King. Excuse my bluntness:
I am a rough straightforward Englishman.

Thomas Proceed straight forward.

Tempter   Purpose is plain.
Endurance of friendship does not depend
Upon ourselves, but upon circumstance.
But circumstance is not undetermined.
Unreal friendship may turn to real
But real friendship, once ended, cannot be mended.
Sooner shall enmity turn to alliance.
The enmity that never knew friendship
Can sooner know accord.

Thomas   For a countryman
You wrap your meaning in as dark generality
As any courtier.

Tempter   This is the simple fact!
You have no hope of reconciliation
With Henry the King. You look only
To blind assertion in isolation.
That is a mistake.

Thomas	O Henry, O my King!
Tempter	Other friends

May be found in the present situation.
King in England is not all-powerful;
King is in France, squabbling in Anjou;
Round him waiting hungry sons.
We are for England. We are in England.
You and I, my Lord, are Normans.
England is a land for Norman
Sovereignty. Let the Angevin
Destroy himself, fighting in Anjou.
He does not understand us, the English barons.
We are the people.

Thomas	To what does this lead?
Tempter	To a happy coalition

Of intelligent interests.

Thomas	But what have you—

If you do speak for barons—

Tempter	For a powerful party

Which has turned its eyes in your direction—
To gain from you, your Lordship asks.
For us, Church favour would be an advantage,
Blessing of Pope powerful protection
In the fight for liberty. You, my Lord,
In being with us, would fight a good stroke,
At once, for England and for Rome,
Ending the tyrannous jurisdiction
Of king's court over bishop's court,
Of king's court over baron's court.

Thomas	which I helped to found
Tempter	Which you helped to found.

But time past is time forgotten.

We expect the rise of a new constellation.

Thomas And if the Archbishop cannot trust the King,
How can he trust those who work for King's undoing?

Tempter Kings will allow no power but their own;
Church and people have good cause against the throne.

Thomas If the Archbishop cannot trust the Throne,
He has good cause to trust none but God alone.
It is not better to be thrown
To a thousand hungry appetites than to one.
At a future time this may be shown.
I ruled once as Chancellor
And men like you were glad to wait at my door.
Not only in the court, but in the field
And in the tilt-yard I made many yield.
Shall I who ruled like an eagle over doves
Now take the shape of a wolf among wolves?
Pursue your treacheries as you have done before:
No one shall say that I betrayed a king.

Tempter Then, my Lord, I shall not wait at your door.
And I well hope, before another spring
The King will show his regard for your loyalty.

Thomas To make, then break, this thought has come before,
The desperate exercise of failing power.
Samson in Gaza did no more.
But if I break, I break myself alone.

The Archbishop walks away from the window
Rays of light pierce heavy black clouds which move slowly across the sky
The Archbishop rises from before the altar in his chapel
His shadow is thrown across the painting above the altar
The Fourth Tempter's voice is heard

The Archbishop walks about his Hall listening to the Fourth Tempter's voice
Sometimes he stops and questions the voice

The modulations on the sound track of the film made by T. S. Eliot's voice speaking the part of the Fourth Tempter.

Fourth Tempter	Well done, Thomas, your will is hard to bend.
	And with me beside you, you shall not lack a friend.
Thomas	Who are you? I expected
	Three visitors, not four.
Tempter	Do not be surprised to receive one more.
	Had I been expected, I had been here before.
	I always precede expectation.
Thomas	Who are you?
Tempter	As you do not know me, I do not need a name,
	And, as you know me, that is why I come.
	You know me, but have never seen my face.
	To meet before was never time or place.
Thomas	Say what you come to say.
Tempter	It shall be said at last.
	Hooks have been baited with morsels of the past.
	Wantonness is weakness. As for the King,
	His hardened hatred shall have no end.
	You know truly, the King will never trust
	Twice, the man who has been his friend.
	Borrow use cautiously, employ
	Your services as long as you have to lend.
	You would wait for trap to snap
	Having served your turn, broken and crushed.
	As for barons, envy of lesser men
	Is still more stubborn than king's anger.
	Kings have public policy, barons private profit,
	Jealously raging possession of the fiend.
	Barons are employable against each other;
	Greater enemies must kings destroy.
Thomas	What is your counsel?

Tempter	Fare forward to the end.

All other ways are closed to you
Except the way already chosen.
But what is pleasure, kingly rule,
Or rule of men beneath a king,
With craft in corners, stealthy stratagem,
To general grasp of spiritual power?
Man oppressed by sin, since Adam fell—
You hold the keys of heaven and hell.
Power to bind and loose: bind, Thomas, bind,
King and bishop under your heel.
King, emperor, bishop, baron, king:
Uncertain mastery of melting armies,
War, plague, and revolution,
New conspiracies, broken pacts;
To be master or servant within an hour,
That is the course of temporal power.
The Old King shall know it, when at last breath.
No sons, no empire, he bites broken teeth.
You hold the skein: wind, Thomas, wind
The thread of eternal life and death.
You hold this power, hold it.

Thomas   Supreme, in this land?

Tempter Supreme, but for one.

Thomas   That I do not understand.

Tempter It is not for me to tell you how this may be so;
I am only here, Thomas, to tell you what you know.

Thomas How long shall this be?

Tempter Save what you know already, ask nothing of me.
But think, Thomas, think of glory after death.
When king is dead, there's another king,
And one more king is another reign.

King is forgotten, when another shall come:
Saint and Martyr rule from the tomb.
Think, Thomas, think of enemies dismayed,
Creeping in penance, frightened of a shade;
Think of pilgrims, standing in line
Before the glittering jewelled shrine,
From generation to generation
Bending the knee in supplication,
Think of the miracles, by God's grace,
And think of your enemies, in another place.

Thomas I have thought of these things.

Tempter   That is why I tell you.
Your thoughts have more power than kings to compel you.
You have also thought, sometimes at your prayers,
Sometimes hesitating at the angles of stairs,
And between sleep and waking, early in the morning,
When the bird cries, have thought of further scorning.
That nothing lasts, but the wheel turns,
The nest is rifled, and the bird mourns;
That the shrine shall be pillaged, and the gold spent,
The jewels gone for light ladies' ornament.
The sanctuary broken, and its stores
Swept into the laps of parasites and whores.
When miracles cease, and the faithful desert you.
And men shall only do their best to forget you.
And later is worse, when men will not hate you
Enough to defame or to execrate you,
But pondering the qualities that you lacked
Will only try to find the historical fact.
When men shall declare that there was no mystery
About this man who played a certain part in history.

68

Thomas   But what is there to do? what is left to be done?
          Is there no enduring crown to be won?
Tempter   Yes, Thomas, yes; you have thought of that too.
          What can compare with glory of Saints
          Dwelling forever in presence of God?
          What earthly glory, of king or emperor,
          What earthly pride, that is not poverty
          Compared with richness of heavenly grandeur?
          Seek the way of martyrdom, make yourself the lowest
          On earth, to be high in heaven.
          And see far off below you, where the gulf is fixed,
          Your persecutors, in timeless torment,
          Parched passion, beyond expiation.
Thomas   No!
          Who are you, tempting with my own desires?
          Others have come, temporal tempters,
          With pleasure and power at palpable price.
          What do you offer? what do you ask?
Tempter   I offer what you desire. I ask
          What you have to give. Is it too much
          For such a vision of eternal grandeur?
Thomas   Others offered real goods, worthless
          But real. You only offer
          Dreams to damnation.
Tempter   You have often dreamt them.
Thomas   Is there no way, in my soul's sickness,
          Does not lead to damnation in pride?
          I well know that these temptations
          Mean present vanity and future torment.
          Can sinful pride be driven out
          Only by more sinful? Can I neither act nor suffer
          Without perdition?

69

The Archbishop is again kneeling at his altar
He bows his head while the Fourth Tempter speaks

Tempter You know and do not know, what it is to act or suffer.
You know and do not know, that action is suffering,
And suffering action. Neither does the agent suffer
Nor the patient act. But both are fixed
In an eternal action, an eternal patience
To which all must consent that it may be willed
And which all must suffer that they may will it,
That the pattern may subsist, that the wheel may turn and
still
Be forever still.

70

The Archbishop still kneels at his altar
A priest comes in through the archway from the Hall and stands
      behind the Archbishop
Two other priests join him

The three Tempters walk into the Chapel
They stand facing the priests
The Archbishop is still kneeling and does not see them
When they have spoken the Tempters turn and walk out through
    the Archbishop's Hall
Two of the priests follow them
The priest who remains goes to the
Archbishop and speaks
The Archbishop does not raise his eyes

A Priest　There is no rest in the house. There is no rest in the street.
I hear restless movement of feet. And the air is heavy and
   thick.
Thick and heavy the sky. And the earth presses up beneath
   my feet.
What is the sickly smell, the vapour? the dark green light
   from a cloud on a withered tree? The earth is heaving
   to parturition of issue of hell. What is the sticky dew
   that forms on the back of my hand?

72

First Tempter	Man's life is a cheat and a disappointment;
	All things are unreal,
	Unreal or disappointing:
Second Tempter	The Catherine wheel, the pantomime cat,
Third Tempter	The prizes given at the children's party,
First Tempter	The prize awarded for the English Essay,
Second Tempter	The scholar's degree, the statesman's decoration.
Third Tempter	All things become less real, man passes
	From unreality to unreality.
	This man is obstinate, blind, intent
	On self-destruction,
	Passing from deception to deception,
	From grandeur to grandeur to final illusion.
	Lost in the wonder of his own greatness,
	The enemy of society, *(The Three Tempters)* enemy of himself.
Third Priest	O Thomas my Lord do not fight the intractable tide,
	Do not sail the irresistible wind; in the storm,
	Should we not wait for the sea to subside, in the night
	Abide the coming of day, when the traveller may find his
	way,
	The sailor lay course by the sun?

The voice of the First Tempter is heard
The First Tempter walks through an archway
He is followed by the Second and the Third Tempters, and by a Priest.

First Tempter Is it the owl that calls, or a signal between the trees?

Second Tempter Is the window-bar made fast, is the door under lock and
bolt?

Third Tempter Is it rain that taps at the window, is it wind that pokes at
the door?

Priest Does the torch flame in the hall, the candle in the room?

First Tempter Does the watchman walk by the wall?

Second Tempter Does the mastiff prowl by the gate?

Third Tempter Death has a hundred hands and walks by a thousand ways.

Priest He may come in the sight of all, he may pass unseen
unheard.

First Tempter Come whispering through the ear, or a sudden shock on
the skull.

Second Tempter A man may walk with a lamp at night, and yet be
drowned in a ditch.

Third Tempter A man may climb the stair in the day, and slip on a broken
step.

Priest A man may sit at meat, and feel the cold in his groin.

The faces of women who speak move slowly past through the shadows

Chorus We have not been happy, my Lord, we have not been too
        happy.
        We are not ignorant women, we know what we must
        expect and not expect.
        We know of oppression and torture.
        We know of extortion and violence,
        Destitution, disease,
        The old without fire in winter,
        The child without milk in summer,
        Our labour taken away from us,
        Our sins made heavier upon us,
        We have seen the young man mutilated,
        The torn girl trembling by the mill-stream.
        And meanwhile we have gone on living,
        Living and partly living,
        Picking together the pieces,
        Gathering faggots at nightfall,
        Building a partial shelter,
        For sleeping, and eating and drinking and laughter.

75

God gave us always some reason, some hope; but now a
    new terror has soiled us, which none can avert, none
    can avoid, flowing under our feet and over the sky;
Under doors and down chimneys, flowing in at the ear
    and the mouth and the eye.
God is leaving us, God is leaving us, more pang, more
    pain than birth or death.
Sweet and cloying through the dark air
Falls the stifling scent of despair;
The forms take shape in the dark air:
Puss-purr of leopard, footfall of padding bear,
Palm-pat of nodding ape, square hyaena waiting
For laughter, laughter, laughter. The Lords of Hell are here.
They curl round you, lie at your feet, swing and wing
    through the dark air.
O Thomas Archbishop, save us, save us, save yourself
    that we may be saved;
Destroy yourself and we are destroyed.

Through the archway leading into his Chapel the Archbishop is seen kneeling at the altar
He rises and a priest comes to take his cloak
The light grows stronger
The Archbishop walks forward and begins to speak

Thomas   Now is my way clear, now is the meaning plain:
Temptation shall not come in this kind again.
The last temptation is the greatest treason:
To do the right deed for the wrong reason.
The natural vigour in the venial sin
Is the way in which our lives begin.
Thirty years ago, I searched all the ways
That lead to pleasure, advancement and praise.
Delight in sense, in learning and in thought,
Music and philosophy, curiosity,
The purple bullfinch in the lilac tree,
The tiltyard skill, the strategy of chess,
Love in the garden, singing to the instrument,
Were all things equally desirable
Ambition comes when early force is spent
And when we find no longer all things possible.
Ambition comes behind and unobservable.
Sin grows with doing good.

77

When I imposed the King's law
In England, and waged war with him against Toulouse,
I beat the barons at their own game. I
Could then despise the men who thought me most
        contemptible,
The raw nobility, whose manners matched their finger-
        nails.
While I ate out of the King's dish
To become servant of God was never my wish.
Servant of God has chance of greater sin
And sorrow, than the man who serves a king.
For those who serve the greater cause may make the cause
        serve them,
Still doing right: and striving with political men
May make that cause political, not by what they do
But by what they are. I know
What yet remains to show you of my history
Will seem to most of you at best futility,
Senseless self-slaughter of a lunatic,
Arrogant passion of a fanatic.
I know that history at all times draws
The strangest consequence from remotest cause.
But for every evil, every sacrilege,
Crime, wrong, oppression and the axe's edge,
Indifference, exploitation, you and you,
And you, must all be punished. So must you.
I shall no longer act or suffer, to the sword's end.
Now my good Angel, whom God appoints
To be my guardian, hover over the swords' points.

A bell is heard ringing
The Archbishop walks up the steps leading out of his Hall

78

The screen is black
The choir is heard
    singing
A carving of the Angel
    appearing to the
    Shepherds slowly
    becomes visible

Laetabundus
Exsultet fidelis chorus,
Alleluia:
Regem Regum
Intactae profudit thorus,
Res miranda.
Angelus consilii
Natus est de Virgine,
Sol de stella:
Sol occasum nesciens,
Stella semper rutilans,
Semper clara.
Sicut sidus radium,
Profert Virgo Filium,
Pari forma.
Neque sidus radio,
Neque Mater filio
Fit corrupta.

The people are coming
    into the crypt for
    Midnight Mass
They hold lighted can-
    dles in their hands
The people kneel
The choir stops singing
    and the people cross
    themselves and get up
The Archbishop stands
    before the altar and
    begins his Christmas
    sermon

INTERLUDE

The Archbishop
preaches in the Cathedral on Christmas Morning, 1170.

'Glory to God in the highest, and on earth peace to men of good will.' *The fourteenth verse of the second chapter of the Gospel according to Saint Luke.* In the Name of the Father, and of the Son, and of the Holy Ghost. Amen.

Dear children of God, my sermon this Christmas morning will be a very short one. I wish only that you should meditate in your hearts the deep meaning and mystery of our masses of Christmas Day. For whenever Mass is said, we re-enact the Passion and Death of Our Lord; and on this Christmas Day we do this in celebration of His Birth. So that at the same moment we rejoice in His coming for the salvation of men, and offer again to God His Body and Blood in sacrifice, oblation and satisfaction for the sins of the whole world. It was in this same night that has just passed, that a multitude of the heavenly host appeared before the shepherds at Bethlehem, saying 'Glory to God in the highest and on earth peace to men of good will'; at this same time of all the year that we celebrate at once the Birth of Our Lord and His Passion and Death upon the Cross. Beloved, as the World sees, this is to behave in a strange fashion. For who in the World will both mourn and rejoice at once and for the same reason? For either joy will be overborne by mourning, or mourning will be cast out by joy; so it is only in these our Christian mysteries that we can rejoice and mourn at once for the same reason. Now think for a moment about the meaning of this word 'peace'. Does it seem strange to you that the angels should have announced Peace, when ceaselessly the world has been stricken with War and the fear of War? Does it seem to you that the angelic voices were mistaken, and that the promise was a disappointment and a cheat?

Reflect now, how Our Lord Himself spoke of Peace. He said to His disciples, 'My peace I leave with you, my peace I give unto you.' Did He mean peace as we think of it: the kingdom of England at peace with its neighbours, the barons at peace with the King, the householder counting over his peaceful gains, the swept hearth, his best wine for a friend at the table, his wife singing to the children? Those men His disciples knew no such things: they went forth to journey afar, to suffer by land and sea, to know torture, imprisonment, disappointment, to suffer death by martyrdom. What then did He mean? If you ask that, remember then that He said also, 'Not as the world gives, give I unto you.' So then, He gave to His disciples peace, but not peace as the world gives.

Consider also one thing of which you have probably never thought. Not only do we at the feast of Christmas celebrate at once Our Lord's Birth and His Death: but on the next day we celebrate the martyrdom of His first martyr, the blessed Stephen. Is it an accident, do you think, that the day of the first martyr follows immediately the day of the Birth of Christ? By no means. Just as we rejoice and mourn at once, in the Birth and in the Passion of Our Lord; so also, in a smaller figure, we both rejoice and mourn in the death of martyrs. We mourn, for the sins of the world that has martyred them; we rejoice, that another soul is numbered among the Saints in Heaven, for the glory of God and for the salvation of men.

Beloved, we do not think of a martyr simply as a good Christian who has been killed because he is a Christian: for that would be solely to mourn. We do not think of him simply as a good Christian who has been elevated to the company of the Saints: for that would be simply to rejoice: and neither our mourning nor our rejoicing is as the world's is. A Christian martyrdom is never an accident. Saints are not made by accident. Still less is a Christian martyrdom the effect of a man's will to become a Saint, as a man by willing and contriving may become a ruler of men. Ambition fortifies the will of man to become a ruler over other men: it operates with deception, cajolery, and violence, it is the action of impurity upon impurity. Not so in Heaven. A martyr, a saint, is always made by the design of God, for His love of men, to warn them and to lead them, to bring them back to His ways. A martyrdom is never the design of man; for the true martyr is he who has become the instrument of God, who has lost his will in the will of God, not lost it but found it, for he has found freedom in submission to God. The martyr no longer desires anything for himself, not even the glory of martyrdom. So thus as on earth the Church mourns and rejoices at once, in a fashion that the world cannot understand; so in Heaven the Saints are most high, having made themselves most low, and are seen, not as we see them, but in the light of the Godhead from which they draw their being.

I have spoken to you to-day, dear children of God, of the martyrs of the past, asking you to remember especially our martyr of Canterbury, the blessed Archbishop Elphege; because it is fitting, on Christ's birth day, to remember what is that Peace which He brought; and because, dear children, I do not think I shall ever preach to you again; and because it is possible that in a short time you may have yet another martyr, and that one perhaps not the last. I would have you keep in your hearts these words that I say, and think of them at another time. In the Name of the Father, and of the Son, and of the Holy Ghost. Amen.

The choir is heard singing
A painting of the Nativity fills the screen

> *Ecce nomen Domini Emmanuel,*
> *Quod annuntiatum est per Gabriel,*
> *Hodie apparuit in Israel:*
> *Per Mariam Virginem est natus Rex.*
> *Eia! Virgo Deum genuit, ut divina voluit clementia*
> *In Bethleem natus est,*
> *Et in Jerusalem visus est,*
> *Et in omnem terram honorificatus est Rex Israel.*

A peasant hut
A donkey stands in its stable and watches
A man comes in carrying wood
His wife stands by the window and speaks to him as he puts the wood down by the fire
She sits down and rocks her child in its cradle

The man sits by the fire warming his hands

     Woman Does the bird sing in the South?
        Man Only the sea-bird cries, driven inland by the storm.
     Woman What sign of the spring of the year?
        Man Only the death of the old: not a stir, not a shoot, not a
              breath.
     Woman Do the days begin to lengthen?
        Man Longer and darker the day, shorter and colder the night.
              Still and stifling the air: but a wind is stored up in the East.
              The starved crow sits in the field, attentive; and in the wood
              The owl rehearses the hollow note of death.
     Woman What signs of a bitter spring?
        Man The wind stored up in the East.
     Woman What, at the time of the birth of Our Lord, at Christmas-
              tide,
              Is there not peace upon earth, goodwill among men?

Man	The peace of this world is always uncertain, unless men keep the peace of God.
	And war among men defiles this world, but death in the Lord renews it,
	And the world must be cleaned in the winter, or we shall have only
	A sour spring, a parched summer, an empty harvest.
Woman	Between Christmas and Easter what work shall be done?
Man	The ploughman shall go out in March and turn the same earth
	He has turned before, the bird shall sing the same song.
Woman	When the leaf is out on the tree, when the elder and may Burst over the stream, and the air is clear and high,
	And voices trill at windows, and children tumble in front of the door,
	What work shall have been done, what wrong
	Shall the bird's song cover, the green tree cover, what wrong
	Shall the fresh earth cover?
Man	We wait, and the time is short But waiting is long.

The woman bends over the child in the cradle

The banner of St. Stephen
The First Priest walks past carrying the banner

First Priest Since Christmas a day: and the day of St. Stephen, First
        Martyr.
Princes moreover did sit, and did witness falsely against me.
A day that was always most dear to the Archbishop
        Thomas.
And he kneeled down and cried with a loud voice:
Lord, lay not this sin to their charge.
Princes moreover did sit.

The banner of St. John the Apostle
The Second Priest walks past carrying the banner

Second Priest   Since St. Stephen a day: and the day of St. John the
               Apostle.
             In the midst of the congregation he opened his mouth.
             That which was from the beginning, which we have
               heard,
             Which we have seen with our eyes, and our hands have
               handled
             Of the word of life; that which we have seen and heard
             Declare we unto you.
             In the midst of the congregation.

87

The banner of the Holy Innocents
The Third Priest walks past carrying the banner

Third Priest Since St. John the Apostle a day: and the day of the Holy
            Innocents.
            Out of the mouths of very babes, O God.
            As the voice of many waters, of thunder, of harps,
            They sung as it were a new song.
            The blood of thy saints have they shed like water,
            And there was no man to bury them. Avenge, O Lord,
            The blood of thy saints. In Rama, a voice heard, weeping.
            Out of the mouths of very babes, O God!

The Priests stand together with the banners behind them.

First Priest　Since the Holy Innocents a day: the fourth day from
　　　　　　　Christmas.

The Three Priests　*Rejoice we all, keeping holy day.*

First Priest　As for the people, so also for himself, he offereth for sins.
　　　　　　　He lays down his life for the sheep.

The Three Priests　*Rejoice we all, keeping holy day.*

First Priest　　　　　　　　　　　To-day?

Second Priest　To-day, what is to-day? For the day is half gone.

First Priest　To-day, what is to-day? but another day, the dusk of the
　　　　　　　year.

Second Priest　To-day, what is to-day? Another night, and another dawn.

Third Priest　What day is the day that we know that we hope for or fear
　　　　　　　for?

　　　　　　　Every day is the day we should fear from or hope from.
　　　　　　　One moment

　　　　　　　Weighs like another. Only in retrospection, selection,

　　　　　　　We say, that was the day. The critical moment

　　　　　　　That is always now, and here. Even now, in sordid
　　　　　　　particulars

　　　　　　　The eternal design may appear.

The three priests walk out
The banner of the Martyrdom of Stephen comes closer and fills the screen

The Archbishop's Hall

A Priest is extinguishing the last candle on the candelabra

A loud knocking is heard

The Third Priest goes to the window and looks out

The First Knight comes to the window and speaks to the Priest
    through the window

The Four Knights come into the Archbishop's Hall and stand in
    front of the priests

First Knight	Servants of the King.
Third Priest	And known to us.
	You are welcome. Have you ridden far?
First Knight	Not far to-day, but matters urgent
	Have brought us from France. We rode hard,
	Took ship yesterday, landed last night,
	Having business with the Archbishop.
Second Knight	Urgent business.
Third Knight	From the King.
Second Knight	By the King's order.
Fourth Knight	Our men are outside.
Third Priest	You know the Archbishop's hospitality.
	We are about to go to dinner.
	The good Archbishop would be vexed
	If we did not offer you entertainment
	Before your business. Please dine with us.
	Your men shall be looked after also.
	Dinner before business. Do you like roast pork?
Fourth Knight	Business before dinner. We will roast your pork
	First, and dine upon it after.
Second Knight	We must see the Archbishop.
Third Knight	Go, tell the Archbishop
	We have no need of his hospitality.
	We will find our own dinner.
Third Priest [to	
Another priest]	Go, tell His Lordship.

The Priest goes out
The Archbishop comes down the steps into his Hall

First Knight	How much longer will you keep us waiting?

The Archbishop advances towards the Knights
He speaks to the Third Priest

  Thomas [*to Priest*] However certain our expectation
                      The moment foreseen may be unexpected
                      When it arrives. It comes when we are
                      Engrossed with matters of other urgency.
                      On my table you will find
                      The papers in order, and the documents signed.

He turns to the Knights

You are welcome, whatever your business may be.
You say, from the King?

First Knight   Most surely from the King.
We must speak with you alone.

Thomas [to Priest]   Leave us then alone.

The Third Priest leaves
The Archbishop turns and walks towards his Chair
The Knights follow him

Now what is the matter?

Second Knight   This is the matter.
You are the Archbishop *(The Four Knights)* in revolt against
    the King; in rebellion to the King and the law of the
    land;
You are the Archbishop who was made by the King;
    whom he set in your place to carry out his command.
You are his servant, his tool, and his jack,
You wore his favours on your back,
You had your honours all from his hand; from him you
    had the power, the seal and the ring.
This is the man who was the tradesman's son: the back-
    stairs brat who was born in Cheapside;
This is the creature that crawled upon the King; swollen
    with blood and swollen with pride.
Creeping out of the London dirt,
Crawling up like a louse on your shirt,
The man who cheated, swindled, lied; broke his oath and
    betrayed his King.

93

Thomas	This is not true.
	Both before and after I received the ring
	I have been a loyal vassal to the King.
	Saving my order, I am at his command,
	As his most faithful vassal in the land.
First Knight	Saving your order! let your order save you—
	As I do not think it is like to do.
	Saving your ambition is what you mean,
	Saving your pride, envy and spleen.
Second Knight	Saving your insolence and greed.
	Won't you ask us to pray to God for you, in your need?
Fourth Knight	Yes, we'll pray for you!
First and Third	
Knights	Yes, we'll pray for you!
The Four Knights	Yes, we'll pray that God may help you!
Thomas	But, gentlemen, your business
	Which you said so urgent, is it only
	Scolding and blaspheming?
First Knight	That was only
	Our indignation, as loyal subjects.
Thomas	Loyal? to whom?
First Knight	To the King!
Second Knight	The King!
Third Knight	The King!
The Four Knights	God bless him!
Thomas	Then let your new coat of loyalty be worn
	Carefully, so it get not soiled or torn.
	Have you something to say?
First Knight	By the King's command.
	Shall we say it now?
Second Knight	Without delay,
	Before the old fox is off and away.

Thomas   What you have to say
             By the King's command—if it be the King's command—
             Should be said in public. If you make charges,
             Then in public I will refute them.
First Knight   No! here and now!
        [*The two priests return at a sign from the Archbishop.*]
    Thomas Now and here!
First Knight Of your earlier misdeeds I shall make no mention,
             They are too well known. But after dissension
             Had ended, in France, and you were endued
             With your former privilege, how did you show your
                 gratitude?
             You had fled from England, not exiled
             Or threatened, mind you; but in the hope
             Of stirring up trouble in the French dominions.
             You sowed strife abroad, you reviled
             The King to the King in France, to the Pope,
             Raising up against him false opinions.
Second Knight Yet the King, out of his charity,
             And urged by your friends, offered clemency,
             Made a pact of peace, and all dispute ended
             Sent you back to your See as you demanded.
 Third Knight And burying the memory of your transgressions
             Restored your honours and your possessions.
             All was granted for which you sued:
             Yet how, I repeat, did you show your gratitude?
 First Knight Suspending those who had crowned the young prince,
             Denying the legality of his coronation.
Second Knight Binding with the chains of anathema.
 Third Knight Using every means in your power to evince
             The King's faithful servants, every one who transacts
             His business in his absence, the business of the nation.

                              95

Second Knight	These are the facts.
	Say therefore if you will be content
	To answer in the King's presence. Therefore were we sent.
Thomas	Never was it my wish
	To uncrown the King's son, or to diminish
	His honour and power. Why should he wish
	To deprive my people of me and keep me from my own
	And bid me sit in Canterbury, alone?
	I would wish him three crowns rather than one,
	And as for the bishops, it is not my yoke
	That is laid upon them, or mine to revoke.
	Let them go to the Pope. It was he who condemned them.
First Knight	Through you they were suspended.
Second Knight	By you be this amended.
Third Knight	Absolve them.
Fourth Knight	Absolve them.
Thomas	I do not deny
	That this was done through me. But it is not I
	Who can loose whom the Pope has bound.
	Let them go to him, upon whom redounds
	Their contempt towards me, their contempt towards the Church shown.
First Knight	Be that as it may, here is the King's command:
	That you and your servants depart from this land.
Thomas	If that *is* the King's command, I will be bold
	To say: seven years were my people without
	My presence; seven years of misery and pain.
	Seven years a mendicant on foreign charity
	I lingered abroad: seven years is no brevity
	I shall not get those seven years back again.
	Never again, you must make no doubt,
	Shall the sea run between the shepherd and his fold.

Second Knight	The King's justice, the King's majesty,
	You insult with gross indignity;
	Insolent madman, whom nothing deters
	From attainting his servants and ministers.
Thomas	It is not I who insult the King,
	And there is higher than I or the King.
	It is not I, Becket from Cheapside,
	It is not against me, Becket, that you strive.
	It is not Becket who pronounces doom,
	But the Law of Christ's Church, the judgement of Rome.
First Knight	Priest, you have spoken in peril of your life.
Second Knight	Priest, you have spoken in danger of the knife.
Third Knight	Priest, you have spoken treachery and treason.
The Four Knights	Priest! traitor, confirmed in malfeasance.
Thomas	I submit my cause to the judgement of Rome.
	But if you kill me, I shall rise from my tomb
	To submit my cause before God's throne.

He goes out.

Fourth Knight	Priest! monk! and servant! take, hold, detain,
	Restrain this man, in the King's name
First Knight	Or answer with your bodies.
Second Knight	Enough of words.
The Four Knights	We come for the King's justice, we come with swords.

The Knights have gone
The Priests close the shutters over the windows
The screen becomes black

The Mary Chapel
Women light candles and place them before the painting of the Virgin
They kneel in front of the candles
One by one they get up and walk away
During this sequence we hear the chorus

> *One Woman* I have smelt them, the death-bringers, senses are quickened
> By subtile forebodings; I have heard

Fluting in the night-time, fluting and owls, have seen at
    noon
Scaly wings slanting over, huge and ridiculous.

Another Woman   I have tasted
The savour of putrid flesh in the spoon. I have felt
The heaving of earth at nightfall, restless, absurd. I have
    heard
Laughter in the noises of beasts that make strange noises:

The Chorus   jackal, jackass, jackdaw; the scurrying noise of mouse
    and jerboa; the laugh of the loon, the lunatic bird.

A Third Woman   I have seen
Grey necks twisting, rat tails twining, in the thick light
    of dawn. I have eaten
Smooth creatures still living, with the strong salt taste of
    living things under sea;

A Fourth Woman   I have tasted the living lobster, the crab, the oyster, the
    whelk and the prawn; and they live and spawn in my
    bowels, and my bowels dissolve in the light of dawn.

A Fifth Woman   I have smelt death in the rose, death in the hollyhock,
    sweet pea, hyacinth, primrose and cowslip

A Sixth Woman   I have seen trunk and horn, tusk and hoof, in odd places;
I have lain on the floor of the sea and breathed with the
    breathing of the sea-anemone, swallowed with
    ingurgitation of the sponge.

A Seventh Woman   I have lain in the soil and criticised the worm. In the air
Flirted with the passage of the kite, I have plunged
    with the kite and cowered with the wren.

An Eighth Woman   I have felt the horn of the beetle, the scale of the viper, the
mobile hard insensitive skin of the elephant, the evasive
flank of the fish.

The Third Woman	I have smelt

The Third Woman   I have smelt
Corruption in the dish, incense in the latrine, the sewer in
the incense, the smell of sweet soap in the woodpath, a
hellish sweet scent in the woodpath, while the ground
heaved.

A Ninth Woman   I have seen
Rings of light coiling downwards, descending
To the horror of the ape. Have I not know, not known
What was coming to be?

A Tenth Woman   It was here, in the kitchen, in the passage,
In the mews in the barn in the byre in the market place

The Chorus   In our veins our bowels our skulls as well
As well as in the plottings of potentates
As well as in the consultations of powers.
What is woven on the loom of fate
What is woven in the councils of princes
Is woven also in our veins, our brains,
Is woven like a pattern of living worms
In the guts of the women of Canterbury.

The Fourth Woman   I have smelt them, the death-bringers, now is too late
For action, too soon for contrition.
Nothing is possible but the shamed swoon
Of those consenting to the last humiliation.

An Eleventh
Woman   I have consented, Lord Archbishop, have consented.

The Chorus   Am torn away, subdued, violated,
United to the spiritual flesh of nature,
Mastered by the animal powers of spirit,
Dominated by the lust of self-demolition,
By the final utter uttermost death of spirit,
By the final ecstasy of waste and shame,

The Tenth Woman O Lord Archbishop, O Thomas Archbishop,
    The Chorus Forgive us, forgive us, pray for us that we may pray for you,
            out of our shame.

The Archbishop appears in the archway leading to the Chapel
The women kneel on the steps before him

        Thomas Peace, and be at peace with your thoughts and visions.
            These things had to come to you and you to accept them.
            This is your share of the eternal burden,
            The perpetual glory. This is one moment,
            But know that another
            Shall pierce you with a sudden painful joy
            When the figure of God's purpose is made complete.
            You shall forget these things, toiling in the household,
            You shall remember them, droning by the fire,
            When age and forgetfulness sweeten memory
            Only like a dream that has often been told
            And often been changed in the telling. They will seem
                unreal.
            Human kind cannot bear very much reality.
            Peace be with you.

The Archbishop blesses the women
The women get up and go back into the Chapel and kneel down
The Archbishop stands watching them
The Priests run towards the Archbishop

Priests My Lord, you must not stop here. To the minster. Through the cloister.

Third Priest No time to waste. They are coming back, armed. To the altar, to the altar.

armed. To the altar, to the altar.

Thomas All my life they have been coming, these feet. All my life I have waited. Death will come only when I am worthy, And if I am worthy, there is no danger. I have therefore only to make perfect my will.

First Priest My Lord, they are coming. They will break through presently.

An Archbishop's You will be killed. Come to the altar.
Knight Make haste, my Lord. Don't stop here talking. It is not right. What shall become of us, my Lord, if you are killed; what shall become of us?

Thomas Peace! be quiet! remember where you are, and what is happening; No life here is sought for but mine, And I am not in danger: only near to death.

A Priest My Lord, to vespers! You must not be absent from vespers.

Third Priest You must not be absent from the divine office. To vespers. Into the cathedral!

Priests Seize him! force him! drag him!

Thomas Keep your hands off!

The Priests seize the Archbishop and drag him away

A face carved on the capital of a pillar
The staring eyes of the face on the pillar
A cloister
The Knights walk drunkenly through the cloister

Another face carved on a pillar
Women appear one after another
Their faces fill the screen
During this sequence we hear the Chorus

Chorus Numb the hand and dry the eyelid,
Still the horror, but more horror
Than when tearing in the belly.

Still the horror, but more horror
Than when twisting in the fingers,
Than when splitting in the skull.

More than footfall in the passage,
More than shadow in the doorway,
More than fury in the hall.

103

The agents of hell disappear, the human, they shrink and
    dissolve
Into dust on the wind, forgotten, unmemorable; only is here
The white flat face of Death, God's silent servant,
And behind the face of death the Judgement
And behind the Judgement the Void, more horrid than
    active shapes of hell;
Emptiness, absence, separation from God;
The horror of the effortless journey, to the empty land
Which is no land, only emptiness, absence the Void,
Where those who were men can no longer turn the mind
To distraction, delusion, escape into dream, pretence,
Where the soul is no longer deceived, for there are no
    objects, no tones,
No colours, no forms to distract, to divert the soul
From seeing itself, foully united forever, nothing with
    nothing,
Not what we call death, but what beyond is death not
    death.
We fear, we fear. Who shall then plead for me,
Who intercede for me, in my most need?

Dead upon the tree, my Saviour,
Let not be in vain Thy labour;
Help me, Lord, in my last fear.

Dust I am, to dust am bending,
From the final doom impending
Help me, Lord, for death is near.

The transept
The Archbishop walks down a flight of steps
The priests are heard shouting
The Archbishop walks to the bottom of the steps and speaks to them

Priests Bar the door. Bar the door.

The door is barred.

We are safe. We are safe.

They dare not break in.

They cannot break in. They have not the force.

We are safe. We are safe.

Thomas Unbar the doors! throw open the doors!

I will not have the house of prayer, the church of Christ,

The sanctuary, turned into a fortress.

The church shall protect her own, in her own way, not

As oak and stone; stone and oak decay,

Give no stay, but the Church shall endure.

The church shall be open, even to our enemies. Open the
    door!

First Priest My Lord! these are not men, these come not as men come,
    but

Like maddened beasts. They come not like men, who

Respect the sanctuary, who kneel to the Body of Christ,

But like beasts. You would bar the door

Against the lion, the leopard, the wolf or the bear,
Why not more
Against beasts with the souls of damned men, against men
Who would damn themselves to beasts. My Lord! My
    Lord!

Thomas You think me reckless, desperate and mad.
You argue by results, as this world does,
To settle if an act be good or bad.
You defer to the fact. For every life and every act
Consequence of good and evil can be shown.
And as in time results of many deeds are blended
So good and evil in the end become confounded.
It is not in time that my death shall be known;
It is out of time that my decision is taken
If you call that decision
To which my whole being gives entire consent.

I give my life
To the Law of God above the Law of Man.
Those who do not the same
How should they know what I do?
How should you know what I do? Yet how much more
Should you know than these madmen beating on the door.
Unbar the door! unbar the door!
We are not here to triumph by fighting, by stratagem, or
    by resistance,
Not to fight with beasts as men. We have fought the beast
And have conquered. We have only to conquer
Now, by suffering. This is the easier victory.
Now is the triumph of the Cross, now
Open the door! I command it. OPEN THE DOOR!

The Knights are heard pounding on the door
The First Priest bows and goes out through an archway
Three other priests follow him
The choir is heard singing the Dies Irae

Three priests run to the Archbishop

     Priests This way, my Lord! Quick. Up the stair. To the roof.
         To the crypt. Quick. Come. Force him.
    Thomas Go to vespers, remember me at your prayers.
        They shall find the shepherd here; the flock shall be spared.
        I have had a tremour of bliss, a wink of heaven, a whisper,
        And I would no longer be denied; all things
        Proceed to a joyful consummation.

The Archbishop blesses the priests
They go out

The knights' voices are heard
They come in through the archway slightly drunk
They see the Archbishop and come towards him speaking together:

108

Knights   Where is Becket, the traitor to the King?
                Where is Becket, the meddling priest?
            Come down Daniel to the lions' den,
                Come down Daniel for the mark of the beast.

            Are you washed in the blood of the Lamb?
                Are you marked with the mark of the beast?
            Come down Daniel to the lions' den,
                Come down Daniel and join in the feast.

            Where is Becket the Cheapside brat?
                Where is Becket the faithless priest?
            Come down Daniel to the lions' den,
                Come down Daniel and join in the feast.

Thomas   It is the just man who
            Like a bold lion, should be without fear.
            I am here.
            No traitor to the King. I am a priest,
            A Christian, saved by the blood of Christ,
            Ready to suffer with my blood.
            This is the sign of the Church always,
            The sign of blood. Blood for blood.
            His blood given to buy my life,
            My blood given to pay for His death,
            My death for His death.

First Knight   Absolve all those you have excommunicated.
Second Knight Resign the powers you have arrogated.
Third Knight   Restore to the King the money you appropriated.
Fourth Knight Renew the obedience you have violated.

Thomas	For my Lord I am now ready to die,
	That his Church may have peace and liberty.
	Do with me as you will, to your hurt and shame;
	But none of my people, in God's name,
	Whether layman or clerk, shall you touch.
	This I forbid.
Knights	Traitor! traitor! traitor!
Thomas	You, Reginald, three times traitor you:
	Traitor to me as my temporal vassal,
	Traitor to me as your spiritual lord,
	Traitor to God in desecrating His Church.
First Knight	No faith do I owe to a renegade,
	And what I owe shall now be paid.

The Archbishop kneels and crosses himself
The Knights stand close behind him

Thomas   Now to Almighty God, to the Blessed Mary, ever Virgin,
to the blessed John the Baptist, the holy apostles Peter
and Paul, to the blessed martyr Denys, and to all the
Saints, I commend my cause and that of the Church.

Dies Irae ends.

The Knights draw their swords and strike the Archbishop
A scream is heard
The Knights strike again
A woman covers her face with her hands

Women appear one after another
Their faces fill the screen
We hear the Chorus:

Chorus   Clear the air! clean the sky! wash the wind! take stone
from stone and wash them.

The land is foul, the water is foul, our beasts and ourselves defiled with blood.

A rain of blood has blinded my eyes. Where is England?
where is Kent? where is Canterbury?

O far far far far in the past; and I wander in a land of
barren boughs: if I break them, they bleed; I wander
in a land of dry stones: if I touch them they bleed.

How, how can I ever return, to the soft quiet seasons?

Night stay with us, stop sun, hold season, let the day not
come, let the spring not come.

Can I look again at the day and its common things, and
see them all smeared with blood, through a curtain
of falling blood?

We did not wish anything to happen.

We understood the private catastrophe,
The personal loss, the general misery,
Living and partly living;
The terror by night that ends in daily action,
The terror by day that ends in sleep;
But the talk in the market-place the hand on the broom,
The night-time heaping of the ashes,
The fuel laid on the fire at daybreak,
These acts marked a limit to our suffering.
Every horror had its definition,
Every sorrow had a kind of end:
In life there is not time to grieve long.
But this, this is out of life, this is out of time,
An instant eternity of evil and wrong.
We are soiled by a filth that we cannot clean, united to
    supernatural vermin,
It is not we alone, it is not the house, it is not the city that
    is defiled,
But the world that is wholly foul.
Clear the air! clean the sky! wash the wind! take the stone
    from the stone, take the skin from the arm, take the
    muscle from the bone, and wash them. Wash the stone,
    wash the bone, wash the brain, wash the soul, wash
    them wash them!

The people run into the Cathedral
An angry crowd surrounds the Knights
The Knights address the crowd

Second Knight Quiet!

I appeal to your sense of justice. As Englishmen you must
hear both sides of the case.

Third Knight In what we have done, whatever you may think of it, we
have been perfectly disinterested. We are not getting
anything out of this. We know perfectly well how
things will turn out. King Henry—God bless him—
will have to say, for reasons of state, that he never
meant this to happen; and at the best we shall have to
spend the rest of our lives abroad.

The people boo.

Shouts for quiet are mixed with the booing.

First Knight You are sensible people, and not to be taken in by
emotional clap-trap. Consider soberly: what were the
Archbishop's aims? and what are King Henry's aims?
Our King wanted to curb the local government because
there was utter chaos; three kinds of justice, three kinds
of courts; that of the King, that of the Bishops, that of
the Barons. While the late Archbishop was Chancellor he supported the King's designs. The King

intended that he should unite the offices of Chancellor
and Archbishop. Had Becket followed the King's
wishes, we should have had an almost ideal state:
a union of spiritual and temporal administration,
under the central government.
But what happened? Becket became more priestly than the
priests. He affirmed there was a higher order than that
which our King, and he as the King's servant, had
for so many years striven to establish; and that—God
knows why—the two orders were incompatible. No
one regrets the necessity for violence more than we do.
Unhappily, there are times when violence is the only
way in which social justice can be secured. At
another time, you would condemn an Archbishop by
vote of Parliament and execute him formally as a

116

traitor. And at a later time still, even such measures as
these would become unnecessary.

The First Knight suddenly stands in darkness
He speaks to the cinema audience

If you have now arrived at a just subordination of the
pretensions of the Church to the welfare of the State,
remember that it is we who took the first step. You
accept our principles; you benefit by our precedent; you
enjoy the fruits of our action. Yet we have been dead
for nearly 800 years and you still call us murderers. In a
moment you will see the Archbishop laid before the
altar and acclaimed as a martyr. Then ask yourselves,
who is more representative of the thing you are: the
man you call a martyr, or the men you call his
murderers?

The screen becomes black
Music is heard
The bell is tolling the knell
The Second Priest carrying the Archbishop's Cross leads a procession through the transept
The priests and Archbishop's Knights carry the Archbishop's bier
The Knights push through the crowd and leave the transept
The people kneel as the procession passes
When the processsion has passed they get up to join it
The Chorus is heard
The Crypt
A monk lights the candles on the altar
The Second Priest leads the procession into the crypt
He lifts the Cross high and places it on the altar
The bier is laid before the altar
The people kneel and bow deeply
Their backs fill the screen

Chorus We praise Thee, O God, for thy glory displayed in all the
creatures of the earth,
In the snow, in the rain, in the wind, in the storm; in all
of Thy creatures, both the hunters and the hunted.
For all things exist only as seen by Thee, only as known by
Thee, all things exist
Only in Thy light, and Thy glory is declared even in that
which denies Thee; the darkness declares the glory
of light.
Those who deny Thee could not deny, if Thou didst not
exist; and their denial is never complete, for if it were
so, they would not exist.
They affirm Thee in living; all things affirm Thee in
living; the bird in the air, both the hawk and the
finch; the beast on the earth, both the wolf and the
lamb; the worm in the soil and the worm in the belly.
Therefore man, whom Thou hast made to be conscious
of Thee, must consciously praise Thee, in thought
and in word and in deed.
Even with the hand to the broom, the back bent in laying
the fire, the knee bent in cleaning the hearth, we, the
scrubbers and sweepers of Canterbury,
The back bent under toil, the knee bent under sin, the
hands to the face under fear, the head bent under grief,
Even in us the voices of seasons, the snuffle of winter, the
song of spring, the drone of summer, the voices of
beasts and of birds, praise Thee.
We thank Thee for Thy mercies of blood, for Thy re-
demption by blood. For the blood of Thy martyrs
and saints
Shall enrich the earth, shall create the holy places.

119

For wherever a saint has dwelt, wherever a martyr has
    given his blood for the blood of Christ,
There is holy ground, and the sanctity shall not depart
    from it
Though armies trample over it, though sightseers come
    with guide-books looking over it;
From where the western seas gnaw at the coast of Iona,
To the death in the desert, the prayer in forgotten places
    by the broken imperial column,
From such ground springs that which forever renews the
    earth
Though it is forever denied. Therefore, O God, we
    thank Thee
Who hast given such blessing to Canterbury.

Forgive us, O Lord, we acknowledge ourselves as type
    of the common man,
Of the men and women who shut the door and sit by the
    fire;
Who fear the blessing of God, the loneliness of the night
    of God, the surrender required, the deprivation
    inflicted;

Who fear the injustice of men less than the justice of God;
Who fear the hand at the window, the fire in the thatch,
    the fist in the tavern, the push into the canal,
Less than we fear the love of God.
We acknowledge our trespass, our weakness, our fault;
    we acknowledge
That the sin of the world is upon our heads; that the
    blood of the martyrs and the agony of the saints
Is upon our heads.

Lord, have mercy upon us.
Christ, have mercy upon us.
Lord, have mercy upon us.
Blessed Thomas, pray for us.

LIST OF ILLUSTRATIONS

ILLUSTRATIONS

COLOUR

MONOCHROME
at the end of the book

125

15. Donald Bisset as the First Priest.

16. Michael Groser as the Third Priest with the Banner of the Holy Innocents.

17. Mark Dignam as the First Knight.

18. Paul Rogers as the Fourth Knight.

19. Leo McKern as the Third Knight.

20. The First Priest.

21. The Second Priest.

22. Arthur Viner as a Blacksmith.

23. David Griffiths as a Blacksmith's boy.

24. Blacksmiths making a sword.

25. Paul Hansard and Anne Cullen as a peasant and his wife.

26. Kay Astor in the Women's Chorus.

27. Ysanne Churchman in the Women's Chorus.

28. Jill Nyasa in the Women's Chorus.

29. Diana Maddox in the Women's Chorus.

30. Louis Karavis as a Blacksmith.

31. Anne Cullen in the Women's Chorus.

32. David Ward as the First Tempter.

33. Becket plays chess with the First Tempter.

34. George Woodbridge as the Second Tempter.

35. The Third Tempter approaches Becket.

36. The Third Priest.

37. Becket addressing his congregation

38. Beryl Calder in the Women's Chorus

39. Renee Bourne-Webb in the Women's Chorus.

40. Michael Aldridge as the Second Knight.

41-48. Sequence of stills from the film negative.

PLATES

8

13

23

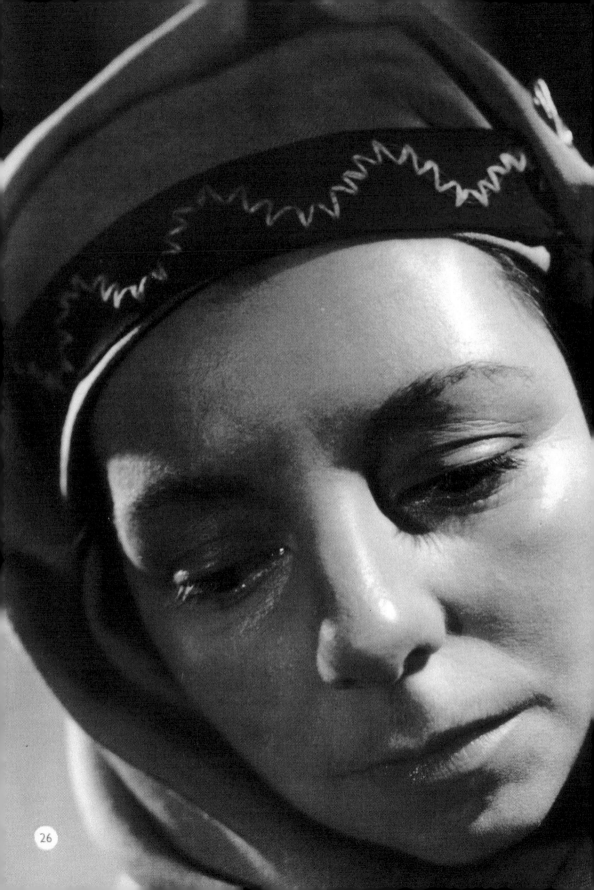

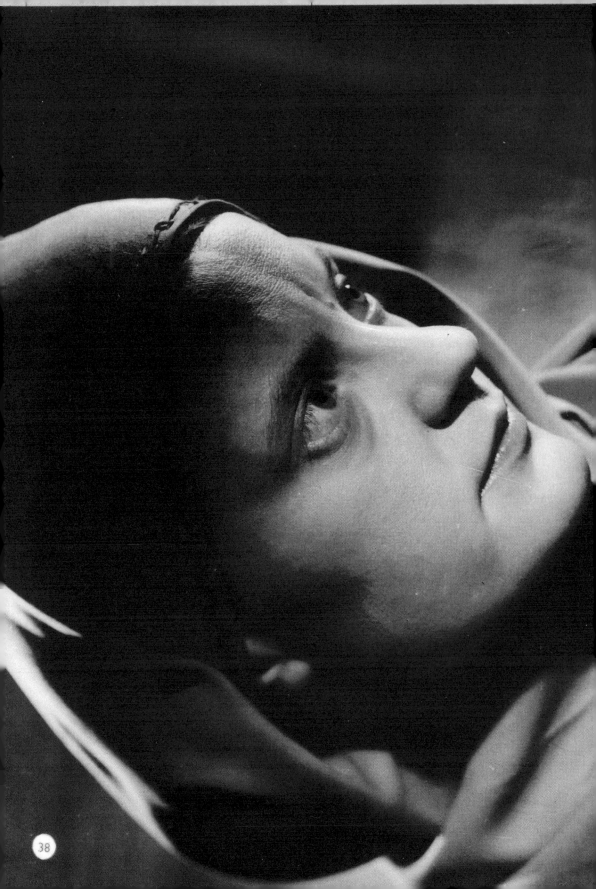

39

The pictures
which follow
are taken
from the
actual film
and are
reproduced here
in the sequence
in which they
come
in the film.
They should be
looked at
from the top
to the bottom
of each column.

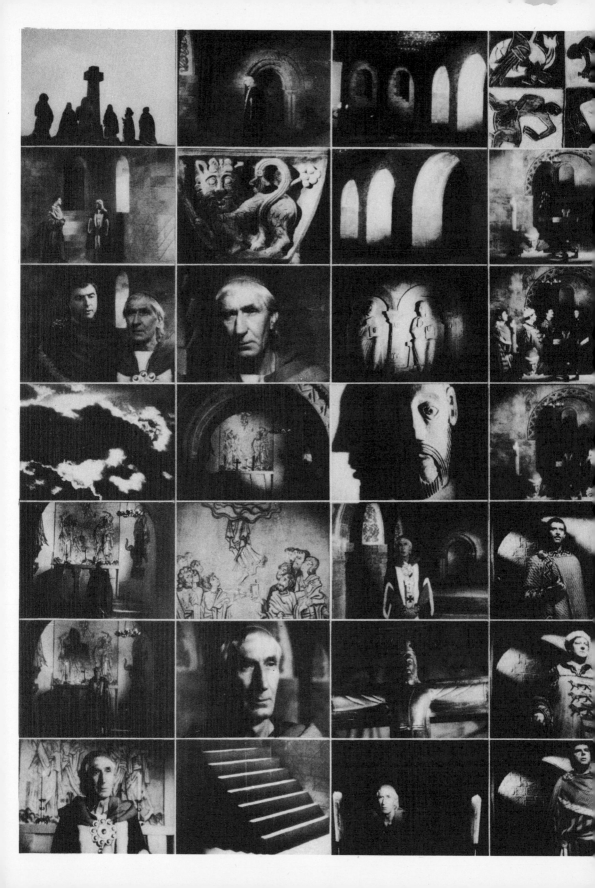